PRIVATE LIVES

An Intimate Comedy in Three Acts

by

NOEL COWARD

GARDEN CITY, NEW YORK

DOUBLEDAY & COMPANY, INC.

Printed in the United States of America

For
JEFFERY
from
NOËL

DRAMATIS PERSONÆ

AMANDA PRYNNE
VICTOR PRYNNE, her husband
LOUISE, a maid
SIBYL CHASE
ELYOT CHASE, her husband

ACT I

The Terrace of a Hotel in France. Summer evening.

ACT II

Amanda's flat in Paris. A few days later. Evening.

ACT III

The same. The next morning.

———

Time: The Present.

ACT I

*The Scene is the terrace of a hotel in France. There
are two French windows at the back opening on
to two separate suites. The terrace space is di-
vided by a line of small trees in tubs, and, down-
stage, running parallel with the footlights, there is
a low stone balustrade. Upon each side of the line
of tree tubs is a set of suitable terrace furniture,
a swinging seat, two or three chairs, and a table.
There are orange and white awnings shading the
windows, as it is summer.*

*When the curtain rises it is about eight o'clock
in the evening. There is an orchestra playing not
very far off. SIBYL CHASE opens the windows on
the Right, and steps out on to the terrace. She
is very pretty and blonde, and smartly dressed in
travelling clothes. She comes down stage, stretches
her arms wide with a little sigh of satisfaction, and
regards the view with an ecstatic expression.*

SIBYL (*calling*):   Elli, Elli dear, do come out. It's so
lovely.

ELYOT (*inside*):   Just a minute.

*After a pause ELYOT comes out. He is about
thirty, quite slim and pleasant looking, and also in
travelling clothes. He walks right down to the*

1

balustrade and looks thoughtfully at the view.
Sibyl *stands beside him, and slips her arm through*
his.

ELYOT: Not so bad.

SIBYL: It's heavenly. Look at the lights of that
yacht reflected in the water. Oh dear, I'm so happy.

ELYOT (*smiling*): Are you?

SIBYL: Aren't you?

ELYOT: Of course I am. Tremendously happy.

SIBYL: Just to think, here we are, you and I, married!

ELYOT: Yes, things have come to a pretty pass.

SIBYL: Don't laugh at me, you mustn't be *blasé*
about honeymoons just because this is your second.

ELYOT (*frowning*): That's silly.

SIBYL: Have I annoyed you by saying that?

ELYOT: Just a little.

SIBYL: Oh, darling, I'm so sorry. (*She holds her*
face up to his.) Kiss me.

ELYOT (*doing so*): There.

SIBYL: Ummm, not so very enthusiastic.

ELYOT (*kissing her again*): That better?

SIBYL: Three times, please, I'm superstitious.

ELYOT (*kissing her*): You really are very sweet.

SIBYL: Are you glad you married me?

ELYOT: Of course I am.

SIBYL: How glad?

ELYOT: Incredibly, magnificently glad.

SIBYL: How lovely.

ELYOT: We ought to go in and dress.

SIBYL: Gladder than before?

ELYOT: Why do you keep harping on that?

SIBYL: It's in my mind, and yours too, I expect.

ELYOT: It isn't anything of the sort.

2

SIBYL: She was pretty, wasn't she? Amanda?

ELYOT: Very pretty.

SIBYL: Prettier than I am?

ELYOT: Much.

SIBYL: Elyot!

ELYOT: She was pretty and sleek, and her hands were long and slim, and her legs were long and slim, and she danced like an angel. You dance very poorly, by the way.

SIBYL: Could she play the piano as well as I can?

ELYOT: She couldn't play the piano at all.

SIBYL (*triumphantly*): Aha! Had she my talent for organisation?

ELYOT: No, but she hadn't your mother either.

SIBYL: I don't believe you like mother.

ELYOT: Like her! I can't bear her.

SIBYL: Elyot! She's a darling, underneath.

ELYOT: I never got underneath.

SIBYL: It makes me unhappy to think you don't like mother.

ELYOT: Nonsense. I believe the only reason you married me was to get away from her.

SIBYL: I married you because I loved you.

ELYOT: Oh dear, oh dear, oh dear, oh dear!

SIBYL: I love you far more than Amanda loved you. I'd never make you miserable like she did.

ELYOT: We made each other miserable.

SIBYL: It was all her fault, you know it was.

ELYOT (*with vehemence*): Yes, it was. Entirely her fault.

SIBYL: She was a fool to lose you.

ELYOT: We lost each other.

SIBYL: She lost you, with her violent tempers and carryings on.

3

ELYOT: Will you stop talking about Amanda?

SIBYL: But I'm very glad, because if she hadn't been uncontrolled, and wicked, and unfaithful, we shouldn't be here now.

ELYOT: She wasn't unfaithful.

SIBYL: How do you know? I bet she was. I bet she was unfaithful every five minutes.

ELYOT: It would take a far more concentrated woman than Amanda to be unfaithful every five minutes.

SIBYL (*anxiously*): You do hate her, don't you?

ELYOT: No, I don't hate her. I think I despise her.

SIBYL (*with satisfaction*): That's much worse.

ELYOT: And yet I'm sorry for her.

SIBYL: Why?

ELYOT: Because she's marked for tragedy; she's bound to make a mess of everything.

SIBYL: If it's all her fault, I don't see that it matters much.

ELYOT: She has some very good qualities.

SIBYL: Considering what a hell she made of your life, I think you are very nice about her. Most men would be vindictive.

ELYOT: What's the use of that? It's all over now, such a long time ago.

SIBYL: Five years isn't very long.

ELYOT (*seriously*): Yes it is.

SIBYL: Do you think you could ever love her again?

ELYOT: Now then, Sibyl.

SIBYL: But could you?

ELYOT: Of course not, I love you.

SIBYL: Yes, but you love me differently; I know that.

ELYOT: More wisely perhaps.

SIBYL: I'm glad. I'd rather have that sort of love.

ELYOT: You're right. Love is no use unless it's wise, and kind, and undramatic. Something steady and sweet, to smooth out your nerves when you're tired. Something tremendously cosy; and unflurried by scenes and jealousies. That's what I want, what I've always wanted really. Oh my dear, I do hope it's not going to be dull for you.

SIBYL: Sweetheart, as tho' you could ever be dull.

ELYOT: I'm much older than you.

SIBYL: Not so very much.

ELYOT: Seven years.

SIBYL (*snuggling up to him*): The music has stopped now and you can hear the sea.

ELYOT: We'll bathe to-morrow morning.

SIBYL: I mustn't get sunburnt.

ELYOT: Why not?

SIBYL: I hate it on women.

ELYOT: Very well, you shan't then. I hope you don't hate it on men.

SIBYL: Of course I don't. It's suitable to men.

ELYOT: You're a completely feminine little creature, aren't you?

SIBYL: Why do you say that?

ELYOT: Everything in its place.

SIBYL: What do you mean?

ELYOT: If you feel you'd like me to smoke a pipe, I'll try and master it.

SIBYL: I like a man to be a man, if that's what you mean.

ELYOT: Are you going to understand me, and manage me?

SIBYL: I'm going to try to understand you.

5

ELYOT: Run me without my knowing it?

SIBYL (*withdrawing slightly*):   I think you're being a little unkind.

ELYOT: No, I don't mean to be. I was only wondering.

SIBYL: Well?

ELYOT: I was wondering what was going on inside your mind, what your plans are really?

SIBYL: Plans; oh, Elli!

ELYOT: Apart from loving me and all that, you must have plans.

SIBYL: I haven't the faintest idea what you're talking about.

ELYOT: Perhaps it's subconscious then, age old instincts working away deep down, mincing up little bits of experience for future use, watching me carefully like a little sharp-eyed, blonde kitten.

SIBYL: How can you be so horrid.

ELYOT: I said Kitten, not Cat.

SIBYL: Kittens grow into cats.

ELYOT: Let that be a warning to you.

SIBYL (*slipping her arm through his again*):   What's the matter, darling; are you hungry?

ELYOT: Not a bit.

SIBYL: You're very strange all of a sudden, and rather cruel. Just because I'm feminine. It doesn't mean that I'm crafty and calculating.

ELYOT: I didn't say you were either of those things.

SIBYL: I hate these half masculine women who go banging about.

ELYOT: I hate anybody who goes banging about.

SIBYL: I should think you needed a little quiet womanliness after Amanda.

ELYOT: Why will you keep on talking about her?

SIBYL: It's natural enough, isn't it?

ELYOT: What do you want to find out?

SIBYL: Why did you really let her divorce you?

ELYOT: She divorced me for cruelty, and flagrant infidelity. I spent a whole week-end at Brighton with a lady called Vera Williams. She had the nastiest looking hair brush I have ever seen.

SIBYL: Misplaced chivalry, I call it. Why didn't you divorce her?

ELYOT: It would not have been the action of a gentleman, whatever that may mean.

SIBYL: I think she got off very lightly.

ELYOT: Once and for all will you stop talking about her.

SIBYL: Yes, Elli dear.

ELYOT: I don't wish to see her again or hear her name mentioned.

SIBYL: Very well, darling.

ELYOT: Is that understood?

SIBYL: Yes, darling. Where did you spend your honeymoon?

ELYOT: St. Moritz. Be quiet.

SIBYL: I hate St. Moritz.

ELYOT: So do I, bitterly.

SIBYL: Was she good on skis?

ELYOT: Do you want to dine downstairs here, or at the Casino?

SIBYL: I love you, I love you, I love you.

ELYOT: Good, let's go in and dress.

SIBYL: Kiss me first.

ELYOT (*kissing her*): Casino?

7

SIBYL: Yes. Are you a gambler? You never told
me.

ELYOT: Every now and then.

SIBYL: I shall come and sit just behind your chair
and bring you luck.

ELYOT: That will be fatal.

*They go off into their suite. There is a slight
pause and then* VICTOR PRYNNE *enters, from the
Left suite. He is quite nice looking, about thirty or
thirty-five. He is dressed in a light travelling suit.
He sniffs the air, looks at the view, and then turns
back to the window.*

VICTOR (*calling*): Mandy.

AMANDA (*inside*): What?

VICTOR: Come outside, the view is wonderful.

AMANDA: I'm still damp from the bath. Wait a
minute——

VICTOR *lights a cigarette. Presently* AMANDA
*comes out on to the terrace. She is quite exquisite
with a gay face and a perfect figure. At the moment she is wearing a negligee.*

I shall catch pneumonia, that's what I shall catch.

VICTOR (*looking at her*): God!

AMANDA: I beg your pardon?

VICTOR: You look wonderful.

AMANDA: Thank you, darling.

VICTOR: Like a beautiful advertisement for something.

AMANDA: Nothing peculiar, I hope.

VICTOR: I can hardly believe it's true. You and I,
here alone together, married!

AMANDA (*rubbing her face on his shoulder*): That
stuff's very rough.

VICTOR: Don't you like it?

8

AMANDA: A bit hearty, isn't it?

VICTOR: Do you love me?

AMANDA: Of course, that's why I'm here.

VICTOR: More than——

AMANDA: Now then, none of that.

VICTOR: No, but do you love me more than you loved Elyot?

AMANDA: I don't remember, it's such a long time ago.

VICTOR: Not so very long.

AMANDA (*flinging out her arms*): All my life ago.

VICTOR: I'd like to break his damned neck.

AMANDA (*laughing*): Why?

VICTOR: For making you unhappy.

AMANDA: It was mutual.

VICTOR: Rubbish! It was all his fault, you know it was.

AMANDA: Yes, it was, now I come to think about it.

VICTOR: Swine!

AMANDA: Don't be so vehement, darling.

VICTOR: I'll never treat you like that.

AMANDA: That's right.

VICTOR: I love you too much.

AMANDA: So did he.

VICTOR: Fine sort of love that is. He struck you once, didn't he?

AMANDA: More than once.

VICTOR: Where?

AMANDA: Several places.

VICTOR: What a cad.

AMANDA: I struck him too. Once I broke four gramophone records over his head. It was very satisfying.

9

VICTOR: You must have been driven to distraction.

AMANDA: Yes, I was, but don't let's talk about it, please. After all, it's a dreary subject for our honeymoon night.

VICTOR: He didn't know when he was well off.

AMANDA: Look at the lights of that yacht reflected in the water. I wonder whose it is.

VICTOR: We must bathe to-morrow.

AMANDA: Yes I want to get a nice sunburn.

VICTOR (*reproachfully*): Mandy!

AMANDA: Why, what's the matter?

VICTOR: I hate sunburnt women.

AMANDA: Why?

VICTOR: It's somehow, well, unsuitable.

AMANDA: It's awfully suitable to me, darling.

VICTOR: Of course if you really want to.

AMANDA: I'm absolutely determined. I've got masses of lovely oil to rub all over myself.

VICTOR: Your skin is so beautiful as it is.

AMANDA: Wait and see. When I'm done a nice crisp brown, you'll fall in love with me all over again.

VICTOR: I couldn't love you more than I do now.

AMANDA: Oh, dear. I did so hope our honeymoon was going to be progressive.

VICTOR: Where did you spend the last one?

AMANDA (*warningly*): Victor.

VICTOR: I want to know.

AMANDA: St. Moritz. It was very attractive.

VICTOR: I hate St. Moritz.

AMANDA: So do I.

VICTOR: Did he start quarrelling with you right away?

AMANDA: Within the first few days. I put it down to the high altitudes.

VICTOR: And you loved him?

AMANDA: Yes, Victor.

VICTOR: You poor child.

AMANDA: You must try not to be pompous, dear. (*She turns away.*)

VICTOR (*hurt*): Mandy!

AMANDA: I don't believe I'm a bit like what you think I am.

VICTOR: How do you mean?

AMANDA: I was never a poor child.

VICTOR: Figure of speech, dear, that's all.

AMANDA: I suffered a good deal, and had my heart broken. But it wasn't an innocent girlish heart. It was jagged with sophistication. I've always been sophisticated, far too knowing. That caused many of my rows with Elyot. I irritated him because he knew I could see through him.

VICTOR: I don't mind how much you see through me.

AMANDA: Sweet. (*She kisses him.*)

VICTOR: I'm going to make you happy.

AMANDA: Are you?

VICTOR: Just by looking after you, and seeing that you're all right, you know.

AMANDA (*a trifle wistfully*): No, I don't know.

VICTOR: I think you love me quite differently from the way you loved Elyot.

AMANDA: Do stop harping on Elyot.

VICTOR: It's true, though, isn't it?

AMANDA: I love you much more calmly, if that's what you mean.

VICTOR: More lastingly?

AMANDA: I expect so.

VICTOR: Do you remember when I first met you?

AMANDA: Yes. Distinctly.

VICTOR: At Marion Vale's party.

AMANDA: Yes.

VICTOR: Wasn't it wonderful?

AMANDA: Not really, dear. It was only redeemed from the completely commonplace by the fact of my having hiccoughs.

VICTOR: I never noticed them.

AMANDA: Love at first sight.

VICTOR: Where did you first meet Elyot?

AMANDA: To hell with Elyot.

VICTOR: Mandy!

AMANDA: I forbid you to mention his name again. I'm sick of the sound of it. You must be raving mad. Here we are on the first night of our honeymoon, with the moon coming up, and the music playing, and all you can do is to talk about my first husband. It's downright sacrilegious.

VICTOR: Don't be angry.

AMANDA: Well, it's very annoying.

VICTOR: Will you forgive me?

AMANDA: Yes; only don't do it again.

VICTOR: I promise.

AMANDA: You'd better go and dress now, you haven't bathed yet.

VICTOR: Where shall we dine, downstairs here, or at the Casino?

AMANDA: The Casino is more fun, I think.

VICTOR: We can play Boule afterwards.

AMANDA: No, we can't, dear.

VICTOR: Don't you like dear old Boule?

AMANDA: No, I hate dear old Boule. We'll play a nice game of Chemin de fer.

VICTOR (*apprehensively*): Not at the big table?

AMANDA: Maybe at the biggest table.

VICTOR: You're not a terrible gambler, are you?

AMANDA: Inveterate. Chance rules my life.

VICTOR: What nonsense.

AMANDA: How can you say it's nonsense. It was chance meeting you. It was chancing falling in love; it's chance that we're here, particularly after your driving. Everything that happens is chance.

VICTOR: You know I feel rather scared of you at close quarters.

AMANDA: That promises to be very embarrassing.

VICTOR: You're somehow different now, wilder than I thought you were, more strained.

AMANDA: Wilder! Oh, Victor, I've never felt less wild in my life. A little strained, I grant you, but that's the newly married atmosphere; you can't expect anything else. Honeymooning is a very overrated amusement.

VICTOR: You say that because you had a ghastly experience before.

AMANDA: There you go again.

VICTOR: It couldn't fail to embitter you a little.

AMANDA: The honeymoon wasn't such a ghastly experience really; it was afterwards that was so awful.

VICTOR: I intend to make you forget it all entirely.

AMANDA: You won't succeed by making constant references to it.

VICTOR: I wish I knew you better.

AMANDA: It's just as well you don't. The "woman"

13

—in italics—should always retain a certain amount of alluring feminine mystery for the "man"—also in italics.

VICTOR: What about the man? Isn't he allowed to have any mystery?

AMANDA: Absolutely none. Transparent as glass.

VICTOR: Oh, I see.

AMANDA: Never mind, darling; it doesn't necessarily work out like that; it's only supposed to.

VICTOR: I'm glad I'm normal.

AMANDA: What an odd thing to be glad about. Why?

VICTOR: Well, aren't you?

AMANDA: I'm not so sure I'm normal.

VICTOR: Oh, Mandy, of course you are, sweetly, divinely normal.

AMANDA: I haven't any peculiar cravings for Chinamen or old boots, if that's what you mean.

VICTOR (*scandalised*): Mandy!

AMANDA: I think very few people are completely normal really, deep down in their private lives. It all depends on a combination of circumstances. If all the various cosmic thingummys fuse at the same moment, and the right spark is struck, there's no knowing what one mightn't do. That was the trouble with Elyot and me, we were like two violent acids bubbling about in a nasty little matrimonial bottle.

VICTOR: I don't believe you're nearly as complex as you think you are.

AMANDA: I don't think I'm particularly complex, but I know I'm unreliable.

VICTOR: You're frightening me horribly. In what way unreliable?

AMANDA: I'm so apt to see things the wrong way round.

VICTOR: What sort of things?

AMANDA: Morals. What one should do and what one shouldn't.

VICTOR (*fondly*): Darling, you're so sweet.

AMANDA: Thank you, Victor, that's most encouraging. You really must have your bath now. Come along.

VICTOR: Kiss me.

AMANDA (*doing so*): There, dear, hurry now; I've only got to slip my dress on and then I shall be ready.

VICTOR: Give me ten minutes.

AMANDA: I'll bring the cocktails out here when they come.

VICTOR: All right.

AMANDA: Go along now, hurry.

> *They both disappear into their suite. After a moment's pause* ELYOT *steps carefully on to the terrace carrying a tray upon which are two champagne cocktails. He puts the tray down on the table.*

ELYOT (*calling*): Sibyl.

SIBYL (*inside*): Yes.

ELYOT: I've brought the cocktails out here, hurry up.

SIBYL: I can't find my lipstick.

ELYOT: Never mind, send down to the kitchen for some cochineal.

SIBYL: Don't be so silly.

ELYOT: Hurry.

> *Elyot saunters down to the balustrade. He looks casually over on to the next terrace, and then out at the view. He looks up at the moon and sighs,*

then he sits down in a chair with his back towards the line of tubs, and lights a cigarette. AMANDA *steps gingerly on to her terrace carrying a tray with two champagne cocktails on it. She is wearing a charmingly simple evening gown, her cloak is flung over her right shoulder. She places the tray carefully on the table, puts her cloak over the back of a chair, and sits down with her back towards* ELYOT. *She takes a small mirror from her handbag, and scrutinizes her face in it. The orchestra downstairs strikes up a new melody. Both* ELYOT *and* AMANDA *give a little start. After a moment,* ELYOT *pensively begins to hum the tune the band is playing. It is a sentimental, romantic little tune.* AMANDA *hears him, and clutches at her throat suddenly as though she were suffocating. Then she jumps up noiselessly, and peers over the line of tubs.* ELYOT, *with his back to her, continues to sing obliviously. She sits down again, relaxing with a gesture almost of despair. Then she looks anxiously over her shoulder at the window in case* VICTOR *should be listening, and then, with a little smile, she takes up the melody herself, clearly.* ELYOT *stops dead and gives a gasp, then he jumps up, and stands looking at her. She continues to sing, pretending not to know that he is there. At the end of the song, she turns slowly, and faces him.*

AMANDA: Thoughtful of them to play that, wasn't it?

ELYOT (*in a stifled voice*): What are you doing here?

AMANDA: I'm on honeymoon.

ELYOT: How interesting, so am I.

AMANDA: I hope you're enjoying it.

ELYOT: It hasn't started yet.

AMANDA: Neither has mine.

ELYOT: Oh, my God!

AMANDA: I can't help feeling that this is a little unfortunate.

ELYOT: Are you happy?

AMANDA: Perfectly.

ELYOT: Good. That's all right, then, isn't it?

AMANDA: Are you?

ELYOT: Ecstatically.

AMANDA: I'm delighted to hear it. We shall probably meet again sometime. Au revoir! (*She turns.*)

ELYOT (*firmly*): Good-bye.

> *She goes indoors without looking back. He stands gazing after her with an expression of horror on his face. SIBYL comes brightly on to the terrace in a very pretty evening frock.*

SIBYL: Cocktail, please. (ELYOT *doesn't answer.*) Elli, what's the matter?

ELYOT: I feel very odd.

SIBYL: Odd, what do you mean, ill?

ELYOT: Yes, ill.

SIBYL (*alarmed*): What sort of ill?

ELYOT: We must leave at once.

SIBYL: Leave!

ELYOT: Yes, dear. Leave immediately.

SIBYL: Elli!

ELYOT: I have a strange foreboding.

SIBYL: You must be mad.

ELYOT: Listen, darling. I want you to be very sweet, and patient, and understanding, and not be upset, or ask any questions, or anything. I have an absolute conviction that our whole future happiness depends upon our leaving here instantly.

SIBYL: Why?

ELYOT: I can't tell you why.

SIBYL: But we've only just come.

ELYOT: I know that, but it can't be helped.

SIBYL: What's happened, what has happened?

ELYOT: Nothing has happened.

SIBYL: You've gone out of your mind.

ELYOT: I haven't gone out of my mind, but I shall if we stay here another hour.

SIBYL: You're not drunk, are you?

ELYOT: Of course I'm not drunk. What time have I had to get drunk?

SIBYL: Come down and have some dinner, darling, and then you'll feel ever so much better.

ELYOT: It's no use trying to humour me. I'm serious.

SIBYL: But, darling, please be reasonable. We've only just arrived; everything's unpacked. It's our first night together. We can't go away now.

ELYOT: We can have our first night together in Paris.

SIBYL: We shouldn't get there until the small hours.

ELYOT (*with a great effort at calmness*): Now please, Sibyl, I know it sounds crazy to you, and utterly lacking in reason and sense, but I've got second sight over certain things. I'm almost psychic. I've got the most extraordinary sensation of impending disaster. If we stay here something appalling will happen. I know it.

SIBYL (*firmly*): Hysterical nonsense.

ELYOT: It isn't hysterical nonsense. Presentiments are far from being nonsense. Look at the woman who cancelled her passage on the *Titanic*. All because of a presentiment.

SIBYL: I don't see what that has to do with it.

ELYOT: It has everything to do with it. She obeyed her instincts, that's what she did, and saved her life. All I ask is to be allowed to obey my instincts.

SIBYL: Do you mean that there's going to be an earthquake or something?

ELYOT: Very possibly, very possibly indeed, or perhaps a violent explosion.

SIBYL: They don't have earthquakes in France.

ELYOT: On the contrary, only the other day they felt a distinct shock at Toulon.

SIBYL: Yes, but that's in the South where it's hot.

ELYOT: Don't quibble, Sibyl.

SIBYL: And as for explosions, there's nothing here that can explode.

ELYOT: Oho, isn't there.

SIBYL: Yes, but, Elli——

ELYOT: Darling, be sweet. Bear with me. I beseech you to bear with me.

SIBYL: I don't understand. It's horrid of you to do this.

ELYOT: I'm not doing anything. I'm only asking you, imploring you to come away from this place.

SIBYL: But I love it here.

ELYOT: There are thousands of other places far nicer.

SIBYL: It's a pity we didn't go to one of them.

ELYOT: Now, listen, Sibyl——

SIBYL: Yes, but why are you behaving like this, why, why, why?

ELYOT: Don't ask why. Just give in to me. I swear I'll never ask you to give in to me over anything again.

SIBYL (*with complete decision*): I won't think of going to-night. It's utterly ridiculous. I've done quite enough travelling for one day, and I'm tired.

ELYOT: You're as obstinate as a mule.

SIBYL: I like that, I must say.

ELYOT (*hotly*): You've got your nasty little feet dug into the ground, and you don't intend to budge an inch, do you?

SIBYL (*with spirit*): No, I do not.

ELYOT: If there's one thing in the world that infuriates me, it's sheer wanton stubbornness. I should like to cut off your head with a meat axe.

SYBYL: How dare you talk to me like that, on our honeymoon night.

ELYOT: Damn our honeymoon night. Damn it, damn it, damn it!

SIBYL (*bursting into tears*): Oh, Elli, Elli——

ELYOT: Stop crying. Will you or will you not come away with me to Paris?

SIBYL: I've never been so miserable in my life. You're hateful and beastly. Mother was perfectly right. She said you had shifty eyes.

ELYOT: Well, she can't talk. Hers are so close together, you couldn't put a needle between them.

SIBYL: You don't love me a little bit. I wish I were dead.

ELYOT: Will you or will you not come to Paris?

SIBYL: No, no I won't.

ELYOT: Oh, my God! (*He stamps indoors.*)

SIBYL (*following him, wailing*): Oh, Elli, Elli, Elli——

VICTOR *comes stamping out of the French windows on the left, followed by* AMANDA.

VICTOR: You were certainly right when you said you weren't normal. You're behaving like a lunatic.

AMANDA: Not at all. All I have done is to ask you a little favour.

VICTOR: Little favour indeed.

AMANDA: If we left now we could be in Paris in a few hours.

VICTOR: If we crossed Siberia by train we could be in China in a fortnight, but I don't see any reason to do it.

AMANDA: Oh, Victor darling—please, please—be sensible, just for my sake.

VICTOR: Sensible!

AMANDA: Yes, sensible. I shall be absolutely miserable if we stay here. You don't want me to be absolutely miserable all through my honeymoon, do you?

VICTOR: But why on earth didn't you think of your sister's tragedy before?

AMANDA: I forgot.

VICTOR: You couldn't forget a thing like that.

AMANDA: I got the places muddled. Then when I saw the Casino there in the moonlight, it all came back to me.

VICTOR: When did all this happen?

AMANDA: Years ago, but it might just as well have been yesterday. I can see her now lying dead, with that dreadful expression on her face. Then all that awful business of taking the body home to England. It was perfectly horrible.

VICTOR: I never knew you had a sister.

AMANDA: I haven't any more.

VICTOR: There's something behind all this.

AMANDA: Don't be silly. What could there be behind it?

VICTOR: Well, for one thing, I know you're lying.

AMANDA: Victor!

VICTOR: Be honest. Aren't you?

AMANDA: I can't think how you can be so mean and suspicious.

VICTOR (*patiently*): You're lying, Amanda. Aren't you?

AMANDA: Yes, Victor.

VICTOR: You never had a sister, dead or alive?

AMANDA: I believe there was a stillborn one in 1902.

VICTOR: What is your reason for all this?

AMANDA: I told you I was unreliable.

VICTOR: Why do you want to leave so badly?

AMANDA: You'll be angry if I tell you the truth.

VICTOR: What is it?

AMANDA: I warn you.

VICTOR: Tell me. Please tell me.

AMANDA: Elyot's here.

VICTOR: What!

AMANDA: I saw him.

VICTOR: When?

AMANDA: Just now, when you were in the bath.

VICTOR: Where was he?

AMANDA (*hesitatingly*): Down there, in a white suit. (*She points over the balustrade.*)

VICTOR (*sceptically*): White suit?

AMANDA: Why not? It's summer, isn't it?

VICTOR: You're lying again.

AMANDA: I'm not. He's here. I swear he is.

VICTOR: Well, what of it?

AMANDA: I can't enjoy a honeymoon with you, with Elyot liable to bounce in at any moment.

VICTOR: Really, Mandy.

AMANDA: Can't you see how awful it is? It's the most embarrassing thing that ever happened to me in my whole life.

VICTOR: Did he see you?

AMANDA: No, he was running.

VICTOR: What was he running for?

AMANDA: How on earth do I know. Don't be so annoying.

VICTOR: Well, as long as he didn't see you it's all right, isn't it?

AMANDA: It isn't right at all. We must leave immediately.

VICTOR: But why?

AMANDA: How can you be so appallingly obstinate.

VICTOR: I'm not afraid of him.

AMANDA: Neither am I. It isn't a question of being afraid. It's just a horrible awkward situation.

VICTOR: I'm damned if I can see why our whole honeymoon should be upset by Elyot.

AMANDA: My last one was.

VICTOR: I don't believe he's here at all.

AMANDA: He is I tell you. I saw him.

VICTOR: It was probably an optical illusion. This half light is very deceptive.

AMANDA: It was no such thing.

VICTOR: I absolutely refuse to change all our plans at the last moment, just because you think you've seen Elyot. It's unreasonable and ridiculous of you to demand it. Even if he is here I can't see that it matters. He'll probably feel much more embarrassed than you, and a damned good job too; and if he annoys you in any way I'll knock him down.

AMANDA: That would be charming.

VICTOR: Now don't let's talk about it any more.

AMANDA: Do you mean to stand there seriously and imagine that the whole thing can be glossed over as easily as that?

VICTOR: I'm not going to leave, Mandy. If I start giving into you as early as this, our lives will be unbearable.

AMANDA (*outraged*): Victor!

VICTOR (*calmly*): You've worked yourself up into a state over a situation which really only exists in your mind.

AMANDA (*controlling herself with an effort*): Please, Victor, please, for this last time I implore you. Let's go to Paris now, to-night. I mean it with all my heart—please——

VICTOR (*with gentle firmness*): No, Mandy!

AMANDA: I see quite clearly that I have been foolish enough to marry a fat old gentleman in a club arm-chair.

VICTOR: It's no use being cross.

AMANDA: You're a pompous ass.

VICTOR (*horrified*): Mandy!

AMANDA (*enraged*): Pompous ass, that's what I said, and that's what I meant. Blown out with your own importance.

VICTOR: Mandy, control yourself.

AMANDA: Get away from me. I can't bear to think I'm married to such rugged grandeur.

VICTOR (*with great dignity*): I shall be in the bar. When you are ready to come down and dine, let me know.

AMANDA (*flinging herself into a chair*): Go away, go away.

VICTOR *stalks off, at the same moment that* ELYOT

stamps on, on the other side, followed by SIBYL
in tears.

ELYOT: If you don't stop screaming, I'll murder you.

SIBYL: I wish to heaven I'd never seen you in my
life, let alone married you. I don't wonder Amanda
left you, if you behaved to her as you've behaved to me.
I'm going down to have dinner by myself and you can
just do what you like about it.

ELYOT: Do, and I hope it chokes you.

SIBYL: Oh Elli, Elli——

She goes wailing indoors. ELYOT *stamps down to
the balustrade and lights a cigarette, obviously
trying to control his nerves.* AMANDA *sees him,
and comes down too.*

AMANDA: Give me one for God's sake.

ELYOT (*hands her his case laconically*):   Here.

AMANDA (*taking a cigarette*):   I'm in such a rage.

ELYOT (*lighting up*):   So am I.

AMANDA: What are we to do?

ELYOT: I don't know.

AMANDA: Whose yacht is that?

ELYOT: The Duke of Westminster's I expect. It
always is.

AMANDA: I wish I were on it.

ELYOT: I wish you were too.

AMANDA: There's no need to be nasty.

ELYOT: Yes there is, every need. I've never in my
life felt a greater urge to be nasty.

AMANDA: And you've had some urges in your time,
haven't you?

ELYOT: If you start bickering with me, Amanda, I
swear I'll throw you over the edge.

AMANDA: Try it, that's all, just try it.

ELYOT: You've upset everything, as usual.

AMANDA: I've upset everything! What about you?

ELYOT: Ever since the first moment I was unlucky enough to set eyes on you, my life has been insupportable.

AMANDA: Oh do shut up, there's no sense in going on like that.

ELYOT: Nothing's any use. There's no escape, ever.

AMANDA: Don't be melodramatic.

ELYOT: Do you want a cocktail? There are two here.

AMANDA: There are two over here as well.

ELYOT: We'll have my two first. (AMANDA *crosses over into* ELYOT's *part of the terrace. He gives her one, and keeps one himself.*)

AMANDA: Shall we get roaring screaming drunk?

ELYOT: I don't think that would help, we did it once before and it was a dismal failure.

AMANDA: It was lovely at the beginning.

ELYOT: You have an immoral memory Amanda. Here's to you. (*They raise their glasses solemnly and drink.*)

AMANDA: I tried to get away the moment after I'd seen you, but he wouldn't budge.

ELYOT: What's his name?

AMANDA: Victor, Victor Prynne.

ELYOT (*toasting*): Mr. and Mrs. Victor Prynne. (*He drinks.*) Mine wouldn't budge either.

AMANDA: What's her name?

ELYOT: Sibyl.

AMANDA (*toasting*): Mr. and Mrs. Elyot Chase. (*She drinks.*) God pity the poor girl.

ELYOT: Are you in love with him?

AMANDA: Of course.

26

ELYOT: How funny.

AMANDA: I don't see anything particularly funny about it, you're in love with yours aren't you?

ELYOT: Certainly.

AMANDA: There you are then.

ELYOT: There we both are then.

AMANDA: What's she like?

ELYOT: Fair, very pretty, plays the piano beautifully.

AMANDA: Very comforting.

ELYOT: How's yours?

AMANDA: I don't want to discuss him.

ELYOT: Well, it doesn't matter, he'll probably come popping out in a minute and I shall see for myself. Does he know I'm here?

AMANDA: Yes, I told him.

ELYOT (*with sarcasm*): That's going to make things a whole lot easier.

AMANDA: You needn't be frightened, he won't hurt you.

ELYOT: If he comes near me I'll scream the place down.

AMANDA: Does Sibyl know I'm here?

ELYOT: No, I pretended I'd had a presentiment. I tried terribly hard to persuade her to leave for Paris.

AMANDA: I tried too, it's lucky we didn't both succeed, isn't it? Otherwise we should probably all have joined up in Rouen or somewhere.

ELYOT (*laughing*): In some frowsy little hotel.

AMANDA (*laughing too*): Oh dear, it would have been much, much worse.

ELYOT: I can see us all sailing down in the morning for an early start.

AMANDA (*weakly*):   Lovely, oh lovely.

ELYOT: Glorious! (*They both laugh helplessly.*)

AMANDA: What's happened to yours?

ELYOT: Didn't you hear her screaming? She's downstairs in the dining-room I think.

AMANDA: Mine is being grand, in the bar.

ELYOT: It really is awfully difficult.

AMANDA: Have you known her long?

ELYOT: About four months, we met in a house party in Norfolk.

AMANDA: Very flat, Norfolk.

ELYOT: How old is dear Victor?

AMANDA: Thirty-four, or five; and Sibyl?

ELYOT: I blush to tell you, only twenty-three.

AMANDA: You've gone a mucker all right.

ELYOT: I shall reserve my opinion of your choice until I've met dear Victor.

AMANDA: I wish you wouldn't go on calling him "Dear Victor." It's extremely irritating.

ELYOT: That's how I see him. Dumpy, and fair, and very considerate, with glasses. Dear Victor.

AMANDA: As I said before I would rather not discuss him. At least I have good taste enough to refrain from making cheap gibes at Sibyl.

ELYOT: You said Norfolk was flat.

AMANDA: That was no reflection on her, unless she made it flatter.

ELYOT: Your voice takes on an acid quality whenever you mention her name.

AMANDA: I'll never mention it again.

ELYOT: Good, and I'll keep off Victor.

AMANDA (*with dignity*):   Thank you.

There is silence for a moment. The orchestra

28

starts playing the same tune that they were sing-ing previously.

ELYOT: That orchestra has a remarkable small repertoire.

AMANDA: They don't seem to know anything but this, do they?

She sits down on the balustrade, and sings it, softly. Her eyes are looking out to sea, and her mind is far away. ELYOT watches her while she sings. When she turns to him at the end, there are tears in her eyes. He looks away awkwardly and lights another cigarette.

ELYOT: You always had a sweet voice, Amanda.

AMANDA (*a little huskily*): Thank you.

ELYOT: I'm awfully sorry about all this, really I am. I wouldn't have had it happen for the world.

AMANDA: I know. I'm sorry too. It's just rotten luck.

ELYOT: I'll go away to-morrow whatever happens, so don't you worry.

AMANDA: That's nice of you.

ELYOT: I hope everything turns out splendidly for you, and that you'll be very happy.

AMANDA: I hope the same for you, too.

The music, which has been playing continually through this little scene, returns persistently to the refrain. They both look at one another and laugh.

ELYOT: Nasty insistent little tune.

AMANDA: Extraordinary how potent cheap music is.

ELYOT: What exactly were you remembering at that moment?

AMANDA: The Palace Hotel Skating Rink in the morning, bright strong sunlight, and everybody whirling round in vivid colours, and you kneeling down to put on my skates for me.

ELYOT: You'd fallen on your fanny a few moments before.

AMANDA: It was beastly of you to laugh like that, I felt so humiliated.

ELYOT: Poor darling.

AMANDA: Do you remember waking up in the morning, and standing on the balcony, looking out across the valley?

ELYOT: Blue shadows on white snow, cleanness beyond belief, high above everything in the world. How beautiful it was.

AMANDA: It's nice to think we had a few marvellous moments.

ELYOT: A few: We had heaps really, only they slip away into the background, and one only remembers the bad ones.

AMANDA: Yes. What fools we were to ruin it all. What utter, utter fools.

ELYOT: You feel like that too, do you?

AMANDA (wearily): Of course.

ELYOT: Why did we?

AMANDA: The whole business was too much for us.

ELYOT: We were so ridiculously over in love.

AMANDA: Funny wasn't it?

ELYOT (sadly): Horribly funny.

AMANDA: Selfishness, cruelty, hatred, possessiveness, petty jealousy. All those qualities came out in us just because we loved each other.

ELYOT: Perhaps they were there anyhow.

AMANDA: No, it's love that does it. To hell with love.

ELYOT: To hell with love.

AMANDA: And yet here we are starting afresh with two quite different people. In love all over again, aren't we? (ELYOT *doesn't answer.*) Aren't we?

ELYOT: No.

AMANDA: Elyot.

ELYOT: We're not in love all over again, and you know it. Good night, Amanda. (*He turns abruptly, and goes towards the French windows.*)

AMANDA: Elyot—don't be silly—come back.

ELYOT: I must go and find Sibyl.

AMANDA: I must go and find Victor.

ELYOT (*savagely*): Well, why don't you?

AMANDA: I don't want to.

ELYOT: It's shameful, shameful of us.

AMANDA: Don't: I feel terrible. Don't leave me for a minute, I shall go mad if you do. We won't talk about ourselves any more, we'll talk about outside things, anything you like, only just don't leave me until I've pulled myself together.

ELYOT: Very well. (*There is a dead silence.*)

AMANDA: What have you been doing lately? During these last years?

ELYOT: Travelling about. I went round the world you know after——

AMANDA (*hurriedly*): Yes, yes, I know. How was it?

ELYOT: The world?

AMANDA: Yes.

ELYOT: Oh, highly enjoyable.

AMANDA: China must be very interesting.

ELYOT: Very big, China.

AMANDA: And Japan——

ELYOT: Very small.

AMANDA: Did you eat sharks' fins, and take your shoes off, and use chopsticks and everything?

ELYOT: Practically everything.

AMANDA: And India, the burning Ghars, or Ghats, or whatever they are, and the Taj Mahal. How was the Taj Mahal?

ELYOT (*looking at her*): Unbelievable, a sort of dream.

AMANDA: That was the moonlight I expect, you must have seen it in the moonlight.

ELYOT (*never taking his eyes off her face*): Yes, moonlight is cruelly deceptive.

AMANDA: And it didn't look like a biscuit box did it? I've always felt that it might.

ELYOT (*quietly*): Darling, darling, I love you so.

AMANDA: And I do hope you met a sacred Elephant. They're lint white I believe, and very, very sweet.

ELYOT: I've never loved anyone else for an instant.

AMANDA (*raising her hand feebly in protest*): No, no, you mustn't—Elyot—stop.

ELYOT: You love me, too, don't you? There's no doubt about it anywhere, is there?

AMANDA: No, no doubt anywhere.

ELYOT: You're looking very lovely you know, in this damned moonlight. Your skin is clear and cool, and your eyes are shining, and you're growing lovelier and lovelier every second as I look at you. You don't hold any mystery for me, darling, do you mind? There isn't a particle of you that I don't know, remember, and want.

AMANDA (*softly*): I'm glad, my sweet.

ELYOT: More than any desire anywhere, deep

down in my deepest heart I want you back again—
please——

AMANDA (*putting her hand over his mouth*): Don't
say any more, you're making me cry so dreadfully.

*He pulls her gently into his arms and they stand
silently, completely oblivious to everything but the
moment, and each other. When finally, they separate, they sit down, rather breathlessly, on the
balustrade.*

AMANDA: What now? Oh, darling, what now?

ELYOT: I don't know, I'm lost, utterly.

AMANDA: We must think quickly, oh quickly——

ELYOT: Escape?

AMANDA: Together?

ELYOT: Yes, of course, now, now.

AMANDA: We can't, we can't, you know we can't.

ELYOT: We must.

AMANDA: It would break Victor's heart.

ELYOT: And Sibyl's too probably, but they're
bound to suffer anyhow. Think of the hell we'd lead
them into if we stayed. Infinitely worse than any
cruelty in the world, pretending to love them, and
loving each other, so desperately.

AMANDA: We must tell them.

ELYOT: What?

AMANDA: Call them, and tell them.

ELYOT: Oh no, no, that's impossible.

AMANDA: It's honest.

ELYOT: I can't help how honest it is, it's too horrible to think of. How should we start? What should
we say?

AMANDA: We should have to trust to the inspiration of the moment.

ELYOT: It would be a moment completely devoid

of inspiration. The most appalling moment imaginable. No, no, we can't, you must see that, we simply can't.

AMANDA: What do you propose to do then? As it is they might appear at any moment.

ELYOT: We've got to decide instantly one way or another. Go away together now, or stay with them, and never see one another again, ever.

AMANDA: Don't be silly, what choice is there?

ELYOT: No choice at all, come— (*He takes her hand.*)

AMANDA: No, wait. This is sheer raving madness, something's happened to us, we're not sane.

ELYOT: We never were.

AMANDA: Where can we go?

ELYOT: Paris first, my car's in the garage, all ready.

AMANDA: They'll follow us.

ELYOT: That doesn't matter, once the thing's done.

AMANDA: I've got a flat in Paris.

ELYOT: Good.

AMANDA: It's in the Avenue Montaigne. I let it to Freda Lawson, but she's in Biarritz, so it's empty.

ELYOT: Does Victor know?

AMANDA: No, he knows I have one but he hasn't the faintest idea where.

ELYOT: Better and better.

AMANDA: We're being so bad, so terribly bad, we'll suffer for this, I know we shall.

ELYOT: Can't be helped.

AMANDA: Starting all those awful rows all over again.

ELYOT: No, no, we're older and wiser now.

AMANDA: What difference does that make? The first moment either of us gets a bit nervy, off we'll go again.

ELYOT: Stop shilly-shallying, Amanda.

AMANDA: I'm trying to be sensible.

ELYOT: You're only succeeding in being completely idiotic.

AMANDA: Idiotic indeed! What about you?

ELYOT: Now look here Amanda——

AMANDA (*stricken*):   Oh my God!

ELYOT (*rushing to her and kissing her*):   Darling, darling, I didn't mean it——

AMANDA: I won't move from here unless we have a compact, a sacred, sacred compact never to quarrel again.

ELYOT: Easy to make but difficult to keep.

AMANDA: No, no, it's the bickering that always starts it. The moment we notice we're bickering, either of us, we must promise on our honour to stop dead. We'll invent some phrase or catchword which when either of us says it, automatically cuts off all conversation for at least five minutes.

ELYOT: Two minutes dear, with an option of renewal.

AMANDA: Very well, what shall it be?

ELYOT (*hurriedly*):   Solomon Isaacs.

AMANDA: All right, that'll do.

ELYOT: Come on, come on.

AMANDA: What shall we do if we meet either of them on the way downstairs?

ELYOT: Run like stags.

AMANDA: What about clothes?

ELYOT: I've got a couple of bags I haven't unpacked yet.

AMANDA: I've got a small trunk.

ELYOT: Send the porter up for it.

AMANDA: Oh this is terrible—terrible——

ELYOT: Come on, come on, don't waste time.

AMANDA: Oughtn't we to leave notes or something?

ELYOT: No, no, no, we'll telegraph from somewhere on the road.

AMANDA: Darling, I daren't, it's too wicked of us, I simply daren't:

ELYOT (*seizing her in his arms and kissing her violently*):   Now will you behave?

AMANDA: Yes, but Elyot darling——

ELYOT: Solomon Isaacs!

They rush off together through ELYOT's *suite. After a moment or so,* VICTOR *steps out on to the terrace and looks round anxiously. Then he goes back indoors again, and can be heard calling "*MANDY.*" Finally he again comes out on to the terrace and comes despondently down to the balustrade. He hears* SIBYL's *voice calling "*ELLI*" and looks round as she comes out of the French windows. She jumps slightly upon seeing him.*

VICTOR: Good evening.

SIBYL (*rather flustered*):   Good-evening—I was—er—looking for my husband.

VICTOR: Really, that's funny. I was looking for my wife.

SIBYL: Quite a coincidence. (*She laughs nervously.*)

VICTOR (*after a pause*):   It's very nice here isn't it?

SIBYL: Lovely.

VICTOR: Have you been here long?

SIBYL: No, we only arrived to-day.

VICTOR: Another coincidence. So did we.

SIBYL: How awfully funny.

VICTOR: Would you care for a cocktail?

SIBYL: Oh no thank you—really——

VICTOR: There are two here on the table.

SIBYL *glances at the two empty glasses on the balustrade, and tosses her head defiantly.*

SIBYL: Thanks very much, I'd love one.

VICTOR: Good, here you are. (SIBYL *comes over to* VICTOR's *side of the terrace. He hands her one and takes one himself.*)

SIBYL: Thank you.

VICTOR (*with rather forced gaiety*): To absent friends. (*He raises his glass.*)

SIBYL (*raising hers*): To absent friends. (*They both laugh rather mirthlessly and then sit down on the balustrade, pensively sipping their cocktails and looking at the view.*) It's awfully pretty isn't it? The moonlight, and the lights of that yacht reflected in the water——

VICTOR: I wonder who it belongs to.

THE CURTAIN SLOWLY FALLS

ACT II

The Scene is AMANDA's *flat in Paris. A few days have elapsed since Act I. The flat is charmingly furnished, its principal features being a Steinway Grand on the Left, facing slightly up stage. Down stage centre, a very large comfortable sofa, behind which is a small table. There is also another sofa somewhere about, and one or two small tables, and a gramophone. The rest can be left to the discretion and taste of the decorator.*

When the Curtain Rises it is about ten o'clock in the evening. The windows are wide open, and the various street sounds of Paris can be heard not very loudly as the apartment is high up.

AMANDA *and* ELYOT *are seated opposite one another at the table. They have finished dinner and are dallying over coffee and liqueurs.* AMANDA *is wearing pajamas, and* ELYOT *a comfortable dressing-gown.*

AMANDA: I'm glad we let Louise go. I am afraid she is going to have a cold.

ELYOT: Going to have a cold; she's been grunting and snorting all the evening like a whole herd of Bison.

AMANDA (*thoughtfully*): Bison never sounds right

38

to me somehow. I have a feeling it ought to be Bisons, a flock of Bisons.

ELYOT: You might say a covey of Bisons, or even a school of Bisons.

AMANDA: Yes, lovely. The Royal London School of Bisons. Do you think Louise is happy at home?

ELYOT: No, profoundly miserable.

AMANDA: Family beastly to her?

ELYOT (*with conviction*):   Absolutely vile. Knock her about dreadfully I expect, make her eat the most disgusting food, and pull her fringe.

AMANDA (*laughing*):   Oh, poor Louise.

ELYOT: Well, you know what the French are.

AMANDA: Oh yes, indeed. I know what the Hungarians are too.

ELYOT: What are they?

AMANDA: Very wistful. It's all those Pretzels I shouldn't wonder.

ELYOT: And the Poostza; I always felt the Poostza was far too big, Danube or no Danube.

AMANDA: Have you ever crossed the Sahara on a Camel?

ELYOT: Frequently. When I was a boy we used to do it all the time. My grandmother had a lovely seat on a Camel.

AMANDA: There's no doubt about it, foreign travel's the thing.

ELYOT: Would you like some brandy?

AMANDA: Just a little. (*He pours some into her glass and some into his own.*)

ELYOT: I'm glad we didn't go out to-night.

AMANDA: Or last night.

ELYOT: Or the night before.

AMANDA: There's no reason to, really, when we're cosy here.

ELYOT: Exactly.

AMANDA: It's nice, isn't it?

ELYOT: Strangely peaceful. It's an awfully bad reflection on our characters. We ought to be absolutely tortured with conscience.

AMANDA: We are, every now and then.

ELYOT: Not nearly enough.

AMANDA: We sent Victor and Sibyl a nice note from wherever it was, what more can they want?

ELYOT: You're even more ruthless than I am.

AMANDA: I don't believe in crying over my bridge before I've eaten it.

ELYOT: Very sensible.

AMANDA: Personally I feel grateful for a miraculous escape. I know now that I should never have been happy with Victor. I was a fool ever to consider it.

ELYOT: You did a little more than consider it.

AMANDA: Well, you can't talk.

ELYOT: I wonder whether they met each other, or whether they've been suffering alone.

AMANDA: Oh dear, don't let's go on about it, it really does make one feel rather awful.

ELYOT: I suppose one or other or both of them will turn up here eventually.

AMANDA: Bound to; it won't be very nice, will it?

ELYOT (*cheerfully*):   Perfectly horrible.

AMANDA: Do you realise that we're living in sin?

ELYOT: Not according to the Catholics, Catholics don't recognise divorce. We're married as much as ever we were.

AMANDA: Yes, dear, but we're not Catholics.

ELYOT: Never mind, it's nice to think they'd sort of

back us up. We were married in the eyes of Heaven, and we still are.

AMANDA: We may be all right in the eyes of Heaven, but we look like being in the hell of a mess socially.

ELYOT: Who cares?

AMANDA: Are we going to marry again, after Victor and Sibyl divorce us?

ELYOT: I suppose so. What do you think?

AMANDA: I feel rather scared of marriage really.

ELYOT: It is a frowsy business.

AMANDA: I believe it was just the fact of our being married, and clamped together publicly, that wrecked us before.

ELYOT: That, and not knowing how to manage each other.

AMANDA: Do you think we know how to manage each other now?

ELYOT: This week's been very successful. We've hardly used Solomon Isaacs at all.

AMANDA: Solomon Isaacs is so long, let's shorten it to Sollocks.

ELYOT: All right.

AMANDA: Darling, you do look awfully sweet in your little dressing-gown.

ELYOT: Yes, it's pretty ravishing, isn't it?

AMANDA: Do you mind if I come round and kiss you?

ELYOT: A pleasure, Lady Agatha.

 AMANDA *comes round the table, kisses him,
 picks up the coffee pot, and returns to her chair.*

AMANDA: What fools we were to subject ourselves to five years' unnecessary suffering.

ELYOT: Perhaps it wasn't unnecessary, perhaps it mellowed and perfected us like beautiful ripe fruit.

41

AMANDA: When we were together, did you really think I was unfaithful to you?

ELYOT: Yes, practically every day.

AMANDA: I thought you were too; often I used to torture myself with visions of your bouncing about on divans with awful widows.

ELYOT: Why widows?

AMANDA: I was thinking of Claire Lavenham really.

ELYOT: Oh Claire.

AMANDA (*sharply*): What did you say "Oh Claire" like that for? It sounded far too careless to me.

ELYOT (*wistfully*): What a lovely creature she was.

AMANDA: Lovely, lovely, lovely!

ELYOT (*blowing her a kiss*): Darling!

AMANDA: Did you ever have an affair with her? Afterwards I mean?

ELYOT: Why do you want to know?

AMANDA: Curiosity, I suppose.

ELYOT: Dangerous.

AMANDA: Oh not now, not dangerous now. I wouldn't expect you to have been celibate during those five years, any more than I was.

ELYOT (*jumping*): What?

AMANDA: After all, Claire was undeniably attractive. A trifle over vivacious I always thought, but that was probably because she was fundamentally stupid.

ELYOT: What do you mean about not being celibate during those five years?

AMANDA: What do you think I mean?

ELYOT: Oh God! (*He looks down miserably.*)

AMANDA: What's the matter?

ELYOT: You know perfectly well what's the matter.

AMANDA (*gently*): You mustn't be unreasonable, I

was only trying to stamp out the memory of you. I expect your affairs well outnumbered mine anyhow.

ELYOT: That is a little different. I'm a man.

AMANDA: Excuse me a moment while I get a caraway biscuit and change my crinoline.

ELYOT: It doesn't suit women to be promiscuous.

AMANDA: It doesn't suit men for women to be promiscuous.

ELYOT (*with sarcasm*): Very modern, dear; really your advanced views quite startle me.

AMANDA: Don't be cross, Elyot, I haven't been so dreadfully loose actually. Five years is a long time, and even if I did nip off with someone every now and again, they were none of them very serious.

ELYOT (*rising from the table and walking away*): Oh, do stop it please——

AMANDA: Well, what about you?

ELYOT: Do you want me to tell you?

AMANDA: No, no, I don't—I take everything back— I don't.

ELYOT (*viciously*): I was madly in love with a woman in South Africa.

AMANDA: Did she have a ring through her nose?

ELYOT: Don't be revolting.

AMANDA: We're tormenting one another. Sit down, sweet, I'm scared.

ELYOT (*slowly*): Very well. (*He sits down thoughtfully.*)

AMANDA: We should have said Sollocks ages ago.

ELYOT: We're in love all right.

AMANDA: Don't say it so bitterly. Let's try to get the best out of it this time, instead of the worst.

ELYOT (*stretching his hand across the table*): Hand please.

AMANDA (*clasping it*): Here.

ELYOT: More comfortable?

AMANDA: Much more.

ELYOT (*after a slight pause*): Are you engaged for this dance?

AMANDA: Funnily enough I was, but my partner was suddenly taken ill.

ELYOT (*rising and going to the gramophone*): It's this damned smallpox epidemic.

AMANDA: No, as a matter of fact it was kidney trouble.

ELYOT: You'll dance it with me I hope?

AMANDA (*rising*): I shall be charmed.

ELYOT (*as they dance*): Quite a good floor, isn't it?

AMANDA: Yes, I think it needs a little Borax.

ELYOT: I love Borax.

AMANDA: Is that the Grand Duchess Olga lying under the piano?

ELYOT: Yes, her husband died a few weeks ago, you know, on his way back from Pulborough. So sad.

AMANDA: What on earth was he doing in Pulborough?

ELYOT: Nobody knows exactly, but there have been the usual stories.

AMANDA: I see.

ELYOT: Delightful parties Lady Bundle always gives, doesn't she?

AMANDA: Entrancing. Such a dear old lady.

ELYOT: And so gay: Did you notice her at supper blowing all those shrimps through her ear trumpet?

    The tune comes to an end. AMANDA *sits on the edge of the sofa, pensively.*

ELYOT: What are you thinking about?

AMANDA: Nothing in particular.

ELYOT: Come on, I know that face.

AMANDA: Poor Sibyl.

ELYOT: Sibyl?

AMANDA: Yes, I suppose she loves you terribly.

ELYOT: Not as much as all that, she didn't have a chance to get really under way.

AMANDA: I expect she's dreadfully unhappy.

ELYOT: Oh, do shut up, Amanda, we've had all that out before.

AMANDA: We've certainly been pretty busy trying to justify ourselves.

ELYOT: It isn't a question of justifying ourselves, it's the true values of the situation that are really important. The moment we saw one another again we knew it was no use going on. We knew it instantly really, although we tried to pretend to ourselves that we didn't. What we've got to be thankful for is that we made the break straight away, and not later.

AMANDA: You think we should have done it anyhow?

ELYOT: Of course, and things would have been in a worse mess than they are now.

AMANDA: And what if we'd never happened to meet again. Would you have been quite happy with Sibyl?

ELYOT: I expect so.

AMANDA: Oh, Elyot!

ELYOT: You needn't look so stricken. It would have been the same with you and Victor. Life would have been smooth, and amicable, and quite charming, wouldn't it?

AMANDA: Poor dear Victor. He certainly did love me.

ELYOT: Splendid.

45

AMANDA: When I met him I was so lonely and depressed, I felt that I was getting old, and crumbling away unwanted.

ELYOT: It certainly is horrid when one begins to crumble.

AMANDA (*wistfully*): He used to look at me hopelessly like a lovely spaniel, and I sort of melted like snow in the sunlight.

ELYOT: That must have been an edifying spectacle.

AMANDA: Victor really had a great charm.

ELYOT: You must tell me all about it.

AMANDA: He had a positive mania for looking after me, and protecting me.

ELYOT: That would have died down in time, dear.

AMANDA: You mustn't be rude, there's no necessity to be rude.

ELYOT: I wasn't in the least rude, I merely made a perfectly rational statement.

AMANDA: Your voice was decidedly bitter.

ELYOT: Victor had glorious legs, hadn't he? And fascinating ears.

AMANDA: Don't be silly.

ELYOT: He probably looked radiant in the morning, all flushed and tumbled on the pillow.

AMANDA: I never saw him on the pillow.

ELYOT: I'm surprised to hear it.

AMANDA (*angrily*): Elyot!

ELYOT: There's no need to be cross.

AMANDA: What did you mean by that?

ELYOT: I'm sick of listening to you yap, yap, yap, yap, yap, yapping about Victor.

AMANDA: Now listen, Elyot, once and for all——

ELYOT: Oh my dear, Sollocks! Sollocks!—two minutes—Sollocks.

AMANDA: But——

ELYOT (*firmly*): Sollocks!

*They sit in dead silence, looking at each other.
AMANDA makes a sign that she wants a cigarette.
ELYOT gets up, hands her the box, and lights one
for her and himself. AMANDA rises and walks over
to the window, and stands there, looking out for a
moment. Presently ELYOT joins her. She slips her
arm through his, and they kiss lightly. They draw
the curtains and then come down and sit side by
side on the sofa. ELYOT looks at his watch. AMANDA
raises her eyebrows at him and he nods, then they
both sigh, audibly.*
That was a near thing.

AMANDA: It was my fault. I'm terribly sorry,
darling.

ELYOT: I was very irritating, I know I was. I'm
sure Victor was awfully nice, and you're perfectly
right to be sweet about him.

AMANDA: That's downright handsome of you.
Sweetheart! (*She kisses him.*)

ELYOT (*leaning back with her on the sofa*): I think
I love you more than ever before. Isn't it ridiculous?
Put your feet up.

*She puts her legs across his, and they snuggle
back together in the corner of the sofa, his head
resting on her shoulder.*

AMANDA: Comfortable?

ELYOT: Almost, wait a minute.

*He struggles a bit and then settles down with a
sigh.*

AMANDA: How long, Oh Lord, how long?

ELYOT (*drowsily*): What do you mean, "How long,
Oh Lord, how long?"

AMANDA: This is far too perfect to last.

ELYOT: You have no faith, that's what's wrong with you.

AMANDA: Absolutely none.

ELYOT: Don't you believe in——? (*He nods upwards.*)

AMANDA: No, do you?

ELYOT (*shaking his head*): No. What about——? (*He points downwards.*)

AMANDA: Oh dear no.

ELYOT: Don't you believe in anything?

AMANDA: Oh yes, I believe in being kind to everyone, and giving money to old beggar women, and being as gay as possible.

ELYOT: What about after we're dead?

AMANDA: I think a rather gloomy merging into everything, don't you?

ELYOT: I hope not, I'm a bad merger.

AMANDA: You won't know a thing about it.

ELYOT: I hope for a glorious oblivion, like being under gas.

AMANDA: I always dream the most peculiar things under gas.

ELYOT: Would you be young always? If you could choose?

AMANDA: No, I don't think so, not if it meant having awful bull's glands popped into me.

ELYOT: Cows for you dear. Bulls for me.

AMANDA: We certainly live in a marvellous age.

ELYOT: Too marvellous. It's all right if you happen to be a specialist at something, then you're too concentrated to pay attention to all the other things going on. But, for the ordinary observer, it's too much.

AMANDA (*snuggling closer*): Far, far too much.

ELYOT: Take the radio for instance.

AMANDA: Oh darling, don't let's take the radio.

ELYOT: Well, aeroplanes then, and Cosmic Atoms, and Television, and those gland injections we were talking about just now.

AMANDA: It must be so nasty for the poor animals, being experimented on.

ELYOT: Not when the experiments are successful. Why in Vienna I believe you can see whole lines of decrepit old rats carrying on like Tiller Girls.

AMANDA (*laughing*): Oh, how very, very sweet.

ELYOT (*burying his face in her shoulder*): I do love you so.

AMANDA: Don't blow, dear heart, it gives me the shivers.

ELYOT (*trying to kiss her*): Swivel your face round a bit more.

AMANDA (*obliging*): That better?

ELYOT (*kissing her lingeringly*): Very nice, thank you kindly.

AMANDA (*twining her arms round his neck*): Darling, you're so terribly, terribly dear, and sweet, and attractive. (*She pulls his head down to her again and they kiss lovingly.*)

ELYOT (*softly*): We were raving mad, ever to part, even for an instant.

AMANDA: Utter imbeciles.

ELYOT: I realised it almost immediately, didn't you?

AMANDA: Long before we got our decree.

ELYOT: My heart broke on that damned trip round the world. I saw such beautiful things, darling. Moonlight shining on old Temples, strange barbaric dances in jungle villages, scarlet Flamingoes flying over deep,

deep blue water. Breathlessly lovely, and completely unexciting because you weren't there to see them with me.

AMANDA (*kissing him again*):   Take me please, take me at once, let's make up for lost time.

ELYOT: Next week?

AMANDA: To-morrow.

ELYOT: Done.

AMANDA: I must see those dear Flamingoes. (*There is a pause.*) Eight years all told, we've loved each other. Three married and five divorced.

ELYOT: Angel. Angel. Angel. (*He kisses her passionately.*)

AMANDA (*struggling slightly*):   No, Elyot, stop now, stop——

ELYOT: Why should I stop? You know you adore being made love to.

AMANDA (*through his kisses*):   It's so soon after dinner.

ELYOT (*jumping up rather angrily*):   You really do say most awful things.

AMANDA (*tidying her hair*):   I don't see anything particularly awful about that.

ELYOT: No sense of glamour, no sense of glamour at all.

AMANDA: It's difficult to feel really glamorous with a crick in the neck.

ELYOT: Why didn't you say you had a crick in your neck?

AMANDA (*sweetly*):   It's gone now.

ELYOT: How convenient. (*He lights a cigarette.*)

AMANDA (*holding out her hand*):   I want one please.

ELYOT (*throwing her one*):   Here.

AMANDA: Match?

ELYOT (*impatiently*): Wait a minute, can't you?

AMANDA: Chivalrous little love.

ELYOT (*throwing the matches at her*): Here.

AMANDA (*coldly*): Thank you very much indeed. (*There is a silence for a moment.*)

ELYOT: You really can be more irritating than anyone in the world.

AMANDA: I fail to see what I've done that's so terribly irritating.

ELYOT: You have no tact.

AMANDA: Tact. You have no consideration.

ELYOT (*walking up and down*): Too soon after dinner indeed.

AMANDA: Yes, much too soon.

ELYOT: That sort of remark shows rather a common sort of mind I'm afraid.

AMANDA: Oh it does, does it?

ELYOT: Very unpleasant, makes me shudder.

AMANDA: Making all this fuss just because your silly vanity is a little upset.

ELYOT: Vanity: What do you mean, vanity?

AMANDA: You can't bear the thought that there are certain moments when our chemical, what d'you call 'ems, don't fuse properly.

ELYOT (*derisively*): Chemical what d'you call 'ems: Please try to be more explicit.

AMANDA: You know perfectly well what I mean, and don't you try to patronise me.

ELYOT (*loudly*): Now look here, Amanda——

AMANDA (*suddenly*): Darling, Sollocks! Oh, for God's sake, Sollocks!

ELYOT: But listen——

AMANDA: Sollocks, Sollocks, Oh dear—triple Sollocks!

They stand looking at one another in silence for a moment, then AMANDA *flings herself down on the sofa and buries her face in the cushions.* ELYOT *looks at her, then goes over to the piano. He sits down and begins to play idly.* AMANDA *raises her head, screws herself round on the sofa, and lies there listening.* ELYOT *blows a kiss to her and goes on playing. He starts to sing softly to her, never taking his eyes off her. When he has finished the little refrain, whatever it was, he still continues to play it looking at her.*

AMANDA: Big romantic stuff, darling.

ELYOT (*smiling*): Yes, big romantic stuff.

He wanders off into another tune. AMANDA *sits up crossed legged on the sofa, and begins to sing it, then, still singing, she comes over and perches on the piano. They sing several old refrains from dead and gone musical comedies finishing with the song that brought them together again in the first Act. Finally* AMANDA *comes down and sits next to him on the piano stool, they both therefore have their backs half turned to the audience. She rests her head on his shoulder, until finally his fingers drop off the keys, and they melt into one another's arms.*

ELYOT (*after a moment*): You're the most thrilling, exciting woman that was ever born.

AMANDA (*standing up, and brushing her hand lightly over his mouth*): Dearest, dearest heart——

He catches at her hand and kisses it, and then her arm, until he is standing up, embracing her ardently. She struggles a little, half laughing, and

*breaks away, but he catches her, and they finish up
on the sofa again, clasped in each other's arms,
both completely given up to the passion of the
moment, until the telephone bell rings violently,
and they both spring apart.*

ELYOT: Good God!

AMANDA: Do you think it's them?

ELYOT: I wonder.

AMANDA: Nobody knows we're here except Freda,
and she wouldn't ring up.

ELYOT: It must be them then.

AMANDA: What are we to do?

ELYOT (*suddenly*):   We're all right, darling, aren't
we—whatever happens?

AMANDA: Now and always, sweet.

ELYOT: I don't care then.

*He gets up and goes defiantly over to the tele-
phone, which has been ringing incessantly during
the little preceding scene.*

AMANDA: It was bound to come sooner or later.

ELYOT (*at telephone*):   Hallo—hallo—what—com-
ment? Madame, qui? 'allo—'allo—oui c'est ca. Oh, Madame Duvallon—Oui, oui, oui. (*He puts his hand over
the mouthpiece.*) It's only somebody wanting to talk
to the dear Madame Duvallon.

AMANDA: Who's she?

ELYOT: I haven't the faintest idea. (*At telephone.*)
Je regrette beaucoup Monsieur, mais Madame Duvallon viens de partir—cette apres midi, pour Madagascar.
(*He hangs up the telepone.*) Whew; that gave me a
fright.

AMANDA: It sent shivers up my spine.

ELYOT: What shall we do if they suddenly walk in
on us?

AMANDA: Behave exquisitely.

ELYOT: With the most perfect poise?

AMANDA: Certainly, I shall probably do a Court Curtsey.

ELYOT (*sitting on the edge of the sofa*): Things that ought to matter dreadfully, don't matter at all when one's happy, do they?

AMANDA: What is so horrible is that one can't stay happy.

ELYOT: Darling, don't say that.

AMANDA: It's true. The whole business is a very poor joke.

ELYOT: Meaning that sacred and beautiful thing, Love?

AMANDA: Yes, meaning just that.

ELYOT (*striding up and down the room dramatically*): What does it all mean, that's what I ask myself in my ceaseless quest for ultimate truth. Dear God, what does it all mean?

AMANDA: Don't laugh at me, I'm serious.

ELYOT (*seriously*): You mustn't be serious, my dear one, it's just what they want.

AMANDA: Who's they?

ELYOT: All the futile moralists who try to make life unbearable. Laugh at them. Be flippant. Laugh at everything, all their sacred shibboleths. Flippancy brings out the acid in their damned sweetness and light.

AMANDA: If I laugh at everything, I must laugh at us too.

ELYOT: Certainly you must. We're figures of fun all right.

AMANDA: How long will it last, this ludicrous, overbearing love of ours?

54

ELYOT: Who knows?

AMANDA: Shall we always want to bicker and fight?

ELYOT: No, that desire will fade, along with our passion.

AMANDA: Oh dear, shall we like that?

ELYOT: It all depends on how well we've played.

AMANDA: What happens if one of us dies? Does the one that's left still laugh?

ELYOT: Yes, yes, with all his might.

AMANDA (*wistfully clutching his hand*):   That's serious enough, isn't it?

ELYOT: No, no, it isn't. Death's very laughable, such a cunning little mystery. All done with mirrors.

AMANDA: Darling, I believe you're talking nonsense.

ELYOT: So is everyone else in the long run. Let's be superficial and pity the poor Philosophers. Let's blow trumpets and squeakers, and enjoy the party as much as we can, like very small, quite idiotic school-children. Let's savour the delight of the moment. Come and kiss me, darling, before your body rots, and worms pop in and out of your eye sockets.

AMANDA: Elyot, worms don't pop.

ELYOT (*kissing her*):   I don't mind what you do see? You can paint yourself bright green all over, and dance naked in the Place Vendome, and rush off madly with all the men in the world, and I shan't say a word, as long as you love me best.

AMANDA: Thank you, dear. The same applies to you, except that if I catch you so much as looking at another woman, I'll kill you.

ELYOT: Do you remember that awful scene we had in Venice?

AMANDA: Which particular one?

ELYOT: The one when you bought that little painted wooden snake on the Piazza, and put it on my bed.

AMANDA: Oh Charles. That was his name, Charles. He did wriggle so beautifully.

ELYOT: Horrible thing, I hated it.

AMANDA: Yes, I know you did. You threw it out of the window into the Grand Canal. I don't think I'll ever forgive you for that.

ELYOT: How long did the row last?

AMANDA: It went on intermittently for days.

ELYOT: The worst one was in Cannes when your curling irons burnt a hole in my new dressing-gown. (*He laughs.*)

AMANDA: It burnt my comb too, and all the towels in the bathroom.

ELYOT: That was a rouser, wasn't it?

AMANDA: That was the first time you ever hit me.

ELYOT: I didn't hit you very hard.

AMANDA: The manager came in and found us rolling on the floor, biting and scratching like panthers. Oh dear, oh dear—— (*She laughs helplessly.*)

ELYOT: I shall never forget his face. (*They both collapse with laughter.*)

AMANDA: How ridiculous, how utterly, utterly ridiculous.

ELYOT: We were very much younger then.

AMANDA: And very much sillier.

ELYOT: As a matter of fact the real cause of that row was Peter Burden.

AMANDA: You knew there was nothing in that.

ELYOT: I didn't know anything of the sort, you took presents from him.

AMANDA: Presents: only a trivial little brooch.

ELYOT: I remember it well, bristling with diamonds. In the worst possible taste.

AMANDA: Not at all, it was very pretty. I still have it, and I wear it often.

ELYOT: You went out of your way to torture me over Peter Burden.

AMANDA: No, I didn't, you worked the whole thing up in your jealous imagination.

ELYOT: You must admit that he was in love with you, wasn't he?

AMANDA: Just a little perhaps. Nothing serious.

ELYOT: You let him kiss you. You said you did.

AMANDA: Well, what of it?

ELYOT: What of it!

AMANDA: It gave him a lot of pleasure, and it didn't hurt me.

ELYOT: What about me?

AMANDA: If you hadn't been so suspicious and nosey you'd never had known a thing about it.

ELYOT: That's a nice point of view I must say.

AMANDA: Oh dear, I'm bored with this conversation.

ELYOT: So am I, bored stiff. (*He goes over to the table.*) Want some brandy?

AMANDA: No thanks.

ELYOT: I'll have a little, I think.

AMANDA: I don't see why you want it, you've already had two glasses.

ELYOT: No particular reason, anyhow they were very small ones.

AMANDA: It seems so silly to go on, and on, and on with a thing.

ELYOT (*pouring himself out a glassful*):   You can

57

hardly call three liqueur glasses in a whole evening going on, and on, and on.

AMANDA: It's become a habit with you.

ELYOT: You needn't be so grand, just because you don't happen to want any yourself at the moment.

AMANDA: Don't be so stupid.

ELYOT (*irritably*): Really, Amanda——

AMANDA: What?

ELYOT: Nothing. AMANDA *sits down on the sofa, and, taking a small mirror from her bag, gazes at her face critically, and then uses some lipstick and powder. A trifle nastily.*) Going out somewhere, dear?

AMANDA: No, just making myself fascinating for you.

ELYOT: That reply has broken my heart.

AMANDA: The woman's job is to allure the man. Watch me a minute will you?

ELYOT: As a matter of fact that's perfectly true.

AMANDA: Oh, no, it isn't.

ELYOT: Yes it is.

AMANDA (*snappily*): Oh be quiet.

ELYOT: It's a pity you didn't have any more brandy; it might have made you a little less disagreeable.

AMANDA: It doesn't seem to have worked such wonders with you.

ELYOT: Snap, snap, snap; like a little adder.

AMANDA: Adders don't snap, they sting.

ELYOT: Nonsense, they have a little bag of venom behind their fangs and they snap.

AMANDA: They sting.

ELYOT: They snap.

AMANDA (*with exasperation*): I don't care, do you understand? I don't care. I don't mind if they bark, and roll about like hoops.

ELYOT (*after a slight pause*):   Did you see much of
Peter Burden after our divorce?

AMANDA: Yes, I did, quite a lot.

ELYOT: I suppose you let him kiss you a good deal
more then.

AMANDA: Mind your own business.

ELYOT: You must have had a riotous time. (AMANDA
doesn't answer, so he stalks about the room.) No re-
straint at all—very enjoyable—you never had much
anyhow.

AMANDA: You're quite insufferable; I expect it's
because you're drunk.

ELYOT: I'm not in the least drunk.

AMANDA: You always had a weak head.

ELYOT: I think I mentioned once before that I have
only had three minute liqueur glasses of brandy the
whole evening long. A child of two couldn't get drunk
on that.

AMANDA: On the contrary, a child of two could get
violently drunk on only one glass of brandy.

ELYOT: Very interesting. How about a child of
four, and a child of six, and a child of nine?

AMANDA (*turning her head away*):   Oh do shut up.

ELYOT (*witheringly*):   We might get up a splendid
little debate about that, you know, Intemperate Tots.

AMANDA: Not very funny, dear; you'd better have
some more brandy.

ELYOT: Very good idea, I will. (*He pours out another glass and gulps it down defiantly.*)

AMANDA: Ridiculous ass.

ELYOT: I beg your pardon?

AMANDA: I said ridiculous ass!

ELYOT (*with great dignity*):   Thank you. (*There

59

is a silence. AMANDA *gets up, and turns the gramophone on.*) You'd better turn that off, I think.

AMANDA (*coldly*): Why?

ELYOT: It's very late and it will annoy the people upstairs.

AMANDA: There aren't any people upstairs. It's a photographer's studio.

ELYOT: There are people downstairs, I suppose?

AMANDA: They're away in Tunis.

ELYOT: This is no time of the year for Tunis. (*He turns the gramophone off.*)

AMANDA (*icily*): Turn it on again, please.

ELYOT: I'll do no such thing.

AMANDA: Very well, if you insist on being boorish and idiotic. (*She gets up and turns it on again.*)

ELYOT: Turn it off. It's driving me mad.

AMANDA: You're far too temperamental. Try to control yourself.

ELYOT: Turn it off.

AMANDA: I won't. (ELYOT *rushes at the gramophone.* AMANDA *tries to ward him off. They struggle silently for a moment then the needle screeches across the record.*) There now, you've ruined the record. (*She takes it off and scrutinises it.*)

ELYOT: Good job, too.

AMANDA: Disagreeable pig.

ELYOT (*suddenly stricken with remorse*): Amanda darling—Sollocks.

AMANDA (*furiously*): Sollocks yourself. (*She breaks the record over his head.*)

ELYOT (*staggering*): You spiteful little beast. (*He slaps her face. She screams loudly and hurls herself sobbing with rage on to the sofa, with her face buried in the cushions.*)

AMANDA (*wailing*): Oh, oh, oh——

ELYOT: I'm sorry, I didn't mean it—I'm sorry, darling, I swear I didn't mean it.

AMANDA: Go away, go away, I hate you. (ELYOT *kneels on the sofa and tries to pull her round to look at him.*)

ELYOT: Amanda—listen—listen——

AMANDA (*turning suddenly, and fetching him a welt across the face*): Listen indeed; I'm sick and tired of listening to you, you damned sadistic bully.

ELYOT (*with great grandeur*): Thank you. (*He stalks towards the door, in stately silence.* AMANDA *throws a cushion at him, which misses him and knocks down a lamp and a vase on the side table.*) (ELYOT *laughs falsely.*) A pretty display I must say.

AMANDA (*wildly*): Stop laughing like that.

ELYOT (*continuing*): Very amusing indeed.

AMANDA (*losing control*): Stop—stop—stop—(*she rushes at him, he grabs her hands and they sway about the room, until he manages to twist her round by the arms so that she faces him, closely, quivering with fury*) —I hate you—do you hear? You're conceited, and overbearing, and utterly impossible!

ELYOT (*shouting her down*): You're a vile tempered loose-living wicked little beast, and I never want to see you again so long as I live.

> *He flings her away from him, she staggers, and falls against a chair. They stand gasping at one another in silence for a moment.*

AMANDA (*very quietly*): This is the end, do you understand? The end, finally and forever.

> *She goes to the door, which opens on to the landing, and wrenches it open. He rushes after her and clutches her wrist.*

ELYOT: You're not going like this.

AMANDA: Oh yes I am.

ELYOT: You're not.

AMANDA: I am; let go of me——(*He pulls her away from the door, and once more they struggle. This time a standard lamp crashes to the floor.* AMANDA, *breathlessly, as they fight.*) You're a cruel fiend, and I hate and loathe you; thank God I've realised in time what you're really like; marry you again, never, never, never. . . . I'd rather die in torment——

ELYOT (*at the same time*): Shut up; shut up. I wouldn't marry you again if you came crawling to me on your bended knees, you're a mean, evil minded, little vampire—I hope to God I never set eyes on you again as long as I live——

> At this point in the proceedings they trip over a piece of carpet, and fall on to the floor, rolling over and over in paroxysms of rage. VICTOR and SIBYL enter quietly, through the open door, and stand staring at them in horror. Finally AMANDA breaks free and half gets up, ELYOT grabs her leg, and she falls against a table, knocking it completely over.

AMANDA (*screaming*): Beast; brute; swine; cad; beast; beast; brute; devil——

> She rushes back at ELYOT who is just rising to his feet, and gives him a stinging blow, which knocks him over again. She rushes blindly off Left, and slams the door, at the same moment that he jumps up and rushes off Right, also slamming the door. VICTOR and SIBYL advance apprehensively into the room, and sink on to the sofa——

THE CURTAIN FALLS

ACT III

*The Scene is the same as Act II. It is the next morning.
The time is about eight-thirty. V*ICTOR *and* S*IBYL
*have drawn the two sofas across the doors Right,
and Left, and are stretched on them, asleep.
V*ICTOR *is in front of* A*MANDA's door, and* S*IBYL in
front of* E*LYOT's.*

*The room is in chaos, as it was left the night
before.*

*As the curtain rises, there is the rattling of a key
in the lock of the front door, and* L*OUISE enters.
She is rather a frowsy looking girl, and carries a
string bag with various bundles of eatables
crammed into it, notably a long roll of bread, and a
lettuce. She closes the door after her, and in the
half light trips over the standard lamp lying on the
floor. She puts her string bag down, and gropes
her way over to the window. She draws the curtains, letting sunlight stream into the room. When
she looks round, she gives a little cry of horror.
Then she sees* V*ICTOR and* S*IBYL sleeping peace-
fully, and comes over and scrutinises each of them
with care, then she shakes* S*IBYL by the shoulder.*

S*IBYL (waking):* Oh dear.
L*OUISE:* Bon jour, Madame.
S*IBYL (bewildered):* What?—Oh—bon jour.

63

LOUISE: Qu'est-ce que vous faites ici, Madame?

SIBYL: What—what?—Wait a moment, attendez un instant—oh dear——

VICTOR (*sleepily*): What's happening? (*Jumping up.*) Of course, I remember now. (*He sees* LOUISE.) Oh!

LOUISE (*firmly*): Bon jour, Monsieur.

VICTOR: Er—bon jour—What time is it?

LOUISE (*rather dully*): Eh, Monsieur?

SIBYL (*sitting up on the sofa*): Quelle heure est il s'il vous plait?

LOUISE: C'est neuf heure moins dix, Madame.

VICTOR: What did she say?

SIBYL: I think she said nearly ten o'clock.

VICTOR (*taking situation in hand*): Er—voulez—er—wake—revillez Monsieur et Madame—er—toute suite?

LOUISE (*shaking her head*): Non, Monsieur. Il m'est absolument defendu de les appeler jusqu'à ce qu'ils sonnent.

> *She takes her bag and goes off into the kitchen.*
> VICTOR *and* SIBYL *look at each other helplessly.*

SIBYL: What are we to do?

VICTOR (*with determination*): Wake them ourselves. (*He goes towards* AMANDA's *door.*)

SIBYL: No, no, wait a minute.

VICTOR: What's the matter?

SIBYL (*plaintively*): I couldn't face them yet, really, I couldn't; I feel dreadful.

VICTOR: So do I. (*He wanders gloomily over to the window.*) It's a lovely morning.

SIBYL: Lovely. (*She bursts into tears.*)

VICTOR (*coming to her*): I say, don't cry.

SIBYL: I can't help it.

VICTOR: Please don't, please——

SIBYL: It's all so squalid, I wish we hadn't stayed; what's the use?

VICTOR: We've got to see them before we go back to England, we must get things straightened out.

SIBYL (*sinking down on to the sofa*):   Oh dear, oh dear, oh dear, I wish I were dead.

VICTOR: Hush, now, hush. Remember your promise. We've got to see this through together and get it settled one way or another.

SIBYL (*sniffling*):   I'll try to control myself, only I'm so . . . so tired, I haven't slept properly for ages.

VICTOR: Neither have I.

SIBYL: If we hadn't arrived when we did, they'd have killed one another.

VICTOR: They must have been drunk.

SIBYL: She hit him.

VICTOR: He'd probably hit her, too, earlier on.

SIBYL: I'd no idea anyone ever behaved like that; it's so disgusting, so degrading, Elli of all people—oh dear——(*She almost breaks down again, but controls herself.*

VICTOR: What an escape you've had.

SIBYL: What an escape we've both had.

> AMANDA *opens her door and looks out. She is wearing travelling clothes, and is carrying a small suitcase. She jumps, upon seeing* SIBYL *and* VIC-TOR.

AMANDA: Oh!—good morning.

VICTOR (*with infinite reproach in his voice*):   Oh, Amanda.

AMANDA: Will you please move this sofa, I can't get out.

> VICTOR *moves the sofa, and she advances into the room and goes towards the door.*

VICTOR: Where are you going?

AMANDA: Away.

VICTOR: You can't.

AMANDA: Why not?

VICTOR: I want to talk to you.

AMANDA (*wearily*):   What on earth is the use of that?

VICTOR: I must talk to you

AMANDA: Well, all I can say is, it's very inconsiderate. (*She plumps the bag down by the door and comes down to* VICTOR.)

VICTOR: Mandy, I——

AMANDA (*gracefully determined to rise above the situation*):   I suppose you're Sibyl; how do you do? (SIBYL *turns her back on her.*) Well, if you're going to take up that attitude, I fail to see the point of your coming here at all.

SIBYL: I came to see Elyot.

AMANDA: I've no wish to prevent you, he's in there, probably wallowing in an alcoholic stupor.

VICTOR: This is all very unpleasant, Amanda.

AMANDA: I quite agree, that's why I want to go away.

VICTOR: That would be shirking; this must be discussed at length.

AMANDA: Very well, if you insist, but not just now, I don't feel up to it. Has Louise come yet?

VICTOR: If Louise is the maid, she's in the kitchen.

AMANDA: Thank you. You'd probably like some coffee, excuse me a moment. (*She goes off into the kitchen.*)

SIBYL: Well! How dare she?

VICTOR (*irritably*):   How dare she what?

SIBYL: Behave so calmly, as though nothing had happened.

VICTOR: I don't see what else she could have done.

SIBYL: Insufferable I call it.

ELYOT *opens his door and looks out.*

ELYOT (*seeing them*): Oh God.

He shuts the door again quickly.

SIBYL: Elyot—Elyot—— (*She rushes over to the door and bangs on it.*) Elyot—Elyot—Elyot——

ELYOT (*inside*): Go away.

SIBYL (*falling on to the sofa*): Oh, oh, oh.

She bursts into tears again.

VICTOR: Do pull yourself together for heaven's sake.

SIBYL: I can't, I can't—oh, oh, oh——

AMANDA *re-enters.*

AMANDA: I've ordered some coffee and rolls, they'll be here soon. I must apologise for the room being so untidy.

> *She picks up a cushion, and pats it into place on the sofa. There is a silence except for* SIBYL's *sobs.* AMANDA *looks at her, and then at* VICTOR; *then she goes off into her room again, and shuts the door.*

VICTOR: It's no use crying like that, it doesn't do any good.

> *After a moment, during which* SIBYL *makes re-newed efforts to control her tears,* ELYOT *opens the door immediately behind her, pushes the sofa, with her on it, out of the way, and walks towards the front door. He is in travelling clothes, and carrying a small suitcase.*

SIBYL (*rushing after him*): Elyot, where are you going?

ELYOT: Canada.

SIBYL: You can't go like this, you can't.

ELYOT: I see no point in staying.

VICTOR: You owe it to Sibyl to stay.

ELYOT: How do you do, I don't think we've met before.

SIBYL: You must stay, you've got to stay.

ELYOT: Very well, if you insist. (*He plumps his bag down.*) I'm afraid the room is in a rather a mess. Have you seen the maid Louise?

VICTOR: She's in the kitchen.

ELYOT: Good. I'll order some coffee.

He makes a movement towards the kitchen.

VICTOR (*stopping him*): No, your—er—my—er—Amanda has already ordered it.

ELYOT: Oh, I'm glad the old girl's up and about.

VICTOR: We've got to get things straightened out, you know.

ELYOT (*looking around the room*): Yes, it's pretty awful. We'll get the concierge up from downstairs.

VICTOR: You're being purposely flippant, but it's no good.

ELYOT: Sorry. (*He lapses into silence.*)

VICTOR (*after a pause*): What's to be done?

ELYOT: I don't know.

SIBYL (*with spirit*): It's all perfectly horrible. I feel smirched and unclean as though slimy things had been crawling all over me.

ELYOT: Maybe they have, that's a very old sofa.

VICTOR: If you don't stop your damned flippancy, I'll knock your head off.

ELYOT (*raising his eyebrows*): Has it ever struck you that flippancy might cover a very real embarrassment?

68

VICTOR: In a situation such as this, it's in extremely bad taste.

ELYOT: No worse than bluster, and invective. As a matter of fact, as far as I know, this situation is entirely without precedent. We have no prescribed etiquette to fall back upon. I shall continue to be flippant.

SIBYL: Oh Elyot, how can you—how can you.

ELYOT: I'm awfully sorry, Sibyl.

VICTOR: It's easy enough to be sorry.

ELYOT: On the contrary. I find it exceedingly difficult. I seldom regret anything. This is a very rare and notable exception, a sort of red letter day. We must all make the most of it.

SIBYL: I'll never forgive you, never. I wouldn't have believed anyone could be so callous and cruel.

ELYOT: I absolutely see your point, and as I said before, I'm sorry.

There is silence for a moment. Then AMANDA *comes in again. She has obviously decided to carry everything off in a high handed manner.*

AMANDA (*in social tones*):   What! Breakfast not ready yet? Really, these French servants are too slow for words. (*She smiles gaily.*) What a glorious morning. (*She goes to the window.*) I do love Paris, it's so genuinely gay. Those lovely trees in the Champs Elysées, and the little roundabouts for the children to play on, and those shiny red taxis. You can see Sacre Cœur quite clearly to-day, sometimes it's a bit misty, particularly in August, all the heat rising up from the pavements you know.

ELYOT (*drily*):   Yes, dear, we know.

AMANDA (*ignoring him*):   And it's heavenly being so high up. I found this flat three years ago, quite by

69

merest chance. I happened to be staying at the Plaza
Athenee, just down the road——

ELYOT (*enthusiastically*): Such a nice hotel, with
the most enchanting courtyard with a fountain that
goes plopplopplopplopplopplopplopplopplop——

VICTOR: This is ridiculous, Amanda.

ELYOT (*continuing*): Plop plop plop plop plop plop
plop plop plop plop——

AMANDA (*overriding him*): Now, Victor, I refuse
to discuss anything in the least important until after
breakfast. I couldn't concentrate now, I know I
couldn't.

ELYOT (*sarcastically*): What manner. What poise.
How I envy it. To be able to carry off the most embarrassing situation with such tact, and delicacy, and
above all—such subtlety. Go on, Amanda, you're making everything so much easier. We shall all be playing
Hunt the Slipper in a minute.

AMANDA: Please don't address me, I don't wish to
speak to you.

ELYOT: Splendid.

AMANDA: And what's more, I never shall again as
long as I live.

ELYOT: I shall endeavour to rise above it.

AMANDA: I've been brought up to believe that it's
beyond the pale, for a man to strike a woman.

ELYOT: A very poor tradition. Certain women
should be struck regularly, like gongs.

AMANDA: You're an unmitigated cad, and a bully.

ELYOT: And you're an ill mannered, bad tempered
slattern.

AMANDA (*loudly*): Slattern indeed.

ELYOT: Yes, slattern, slattern, slattern, and fishwife.

VICTOR: Keep your mouth shut, you swine.

ELYOT: Mind your own damned business.

They are about to fight, when SIBYL *rushes between them.*

SIBYL: Stop, stop, it's no use going on like this. Stop, please. (*To* AMANDA) Help me, do, do, do, help me——

AMANDA: I'm not going to interfere. Let them fight if they want to, it will probably clear the air anyhow.

SIBYL: Yes but——

AMANDA: Come into my room, perhaps you'd like to wash or something.

SIBYL: No, but——

AMANDA (*firmly*): Come along.

SIBYL: Very well.

She tosses her head at ELYOT, *and* AMANDA *drags her off.*

VICTOR (*belligerently*): Now then!

ELYOT: Now then what?

VICTOR: Are you going to take back those things you said to Amanda?

ELYOT: Certainly, I'll take back anything, if only you'll stop bellowing at me.

VICTOR (*contemptuously*): You're a coward too.

ELYOT: They want us to fight, don't you see?

VICTOR: No, I don't, why should they?

ELYOT: Primitive feminine instincts—warring males—very enjoyable.

VICTOR: You think you're very clever, don't you?

ELYOT: I think I'm a bit cleverer than you, but apparently that's not saying much.

VICTOR (*violently*): What?

ELYOT: Oh, do sit down.

VICTOR: I will not.

ELYOT: Well, if you'll excuse me, I will, I'm extremely tired.

He sits down.

VICTOR: Oh, for God's sake, behave like a man.

ELYOT (*patiently*): Listen a minute, all this belligerency is very right and proper and highly traditional, but if only you'll think for a moment, you'll see that it won't get us very far.

VICTOR: To hell with all that.

ELYOT: I should like to explain that if you hit me, I shall certainly hit you, probably equally hard, if not harder. I'm just as strong as you I should imagine. Then you'd hit me again, and I'd hit you again, and we'd go on until one or the other was knocked out. Now if you'll explain to me satisfactorily how all that can possibly improve the situation, I'll tear off my coat, and we'll go at one another hammer and tongs, immediately.

VICTOR: It would ease my mind.

ELYOT: Only if you won.

VICTOR: I should win all right.

ELYOT: Want to try?

VICTOR: Yes.

ELYOT (*jumping up*): Here goes then——

He tears off his coat.

VICTOR: Just a moment.

ELYOT: Well?

VICTOR: What did you mean about them wanting us to fight?

ELYOT: It would be balm to their vanity.

VICTOR: Do you love Amanda?

ELYOT: Is this a battle or a discussion? If it's the latter I shall put on my coat again, I don't want to catch a chill.

VICTOR: Answer my question, please.

ELYOT: Have a cigarette?

VICTOR (*stormily*):   Answer my question.

ELYOT: If you analyse it, it's rather a silly question.

VICTOR: Do you love Amanda?

ELYOT (*confidentially*):   Not very much this morning, to be perfectly frank, I'd like to wring her neck. Do you love her?

VICTOR: That's beside the point.

ELYOT: On the contrary, it's the crux of the whole affair. If you do love her still, you can forgive her, and live with her in peace and harmony until you're ninety-eight.

VICTOR: You're apparently even more of a cad than I thought you were.

ELYOT: You are completely in the right over the whole business, don't imagine I'm not perfectly conscious of that.

VICTOR: I'm glad.

ELYOT: It's all very unfortunate.

VICTOR: Unfortunate: My God!

ELYOT: It might have been worse.

VICTOR: I'm glad you think so.

ELYOT: I do wish you'd stop about being so glad about everything.

VICTOR: What do you intend to do? That's what I want to know. What do you intend to do?

ELYOT (*suddenly serious*):   I don't know, I don't care.

VICTOR: I suppose you realise that you've broken that poor little woman's heart?

ELYOT: Which poor little woman?

VICTOR: Sibyl, of course.

ELYOT: Oh, come now, not as bad as that. She'll get over it, and forget all about me.

VICTOR: I sincerely hope so . . . for her sake.

ELYOT: Amanda will forget all about me too. Everybody will forget all about me. I might just as well lie down and die in fearful pain and suffering, nobody would care.

VICTOR: Don't talk such rot.

ELYOT: You must forgive me for taking rather a gloomy view of everything but the fact is, I suddenly feel slightly depressed.

VICTOR: I intend to divorce Amanda, naming you as co-respondent.

ELYOT: Very well.

VICTOR: And Sibyl will divorce you for Amanda. It would be foolish of either of you to attempt any defence.

ELYOT: Quite.

VICTOR: And the sooner you marry Amanda again, the better.

ELYOT: I'm not going to marry Amanda.

VICTOR: What?

ELYOT: She's a vile tempered wicked woman.

VICTOR: You should have thought of that before.

ELYOT: I did think of it before.

VICTOR (firmly): You've got to marry her.

ELYOT: I'd rather marry a ravening Leopard.

VICTOR (angrily): Now look here. I'm sick of all this shilly-shallying. You're getting off a good deal more lightly than you deserve; you can consider yourself damned lucky I didn't shoot you.

ELYOT (with sudden vehemence): Well, if you'd had a spark of manliness in you, you would have shot me. You're all fuss and fume, one of these cotton wool Englishmen. I despise you.

VICTOR (*through clenched teeth*):   You despise me?

ELYOT: Yes, utterly. You're nothing but a rampaging gas bag! (*He goes off into his room and slams the door, leaving* VICTOR *speechless with fury,* AMANDA *and* SIBYL *re-enter.*)

AMANDA (*brightly*):   Well, what's happened?

VICTOR (*sullenly*):   Nothing's happened.

AMANDA: You ought to be ashamed to admit it.

SIBYL: Where's Elyot?

VICTOR: In there.

AMANDA: What's he doing?

VICTOR (*turning angrily away*):   How do I know what he's doing?

AMANDA: If you were half the man I thought you were, he'd be bandaging himself.

SIBYL (*with defiance*):   Elyot's just as strong as Victor.

AMANDA (*savagely*):   I should like it proved.

SIBYL: There's no need to be so vindictive.

AMANDA: You were abusing Elyot like a pickpocket to me a little while ago, now you are standing up for him.

SIBYL: I'm beginning to suspect that he wasn't quite so much to blame as I thought.

AMANDA: Oh really?

SIBYL: You certainly have a very unpleasant temper.

AMANDA: It's a little difficult to keep up with your rapid changes of front, but you're young and inexperienced, so I forgive you freely.

SIBYL (*heatedly*):   Seeing the depths of degrada-

tion to which age and experience have brought you,
I'm glad I'm as I am!

AMANDA (*with great grandeur*):   That was exceedingly rude. I think you'd better go away somewhere.
(*She waves her hand vaguely.*)

SIBYL: After all, Elyot is my husband.

AMANDA: Take him with you, by all means.

SIBYL: If you're not very careful, I will! (*She goes
over to* ELYOT's *door and bangs on it.*) Elyot—
Elyot——

ELYOT (*inside*):   What is it?

SIBYL: Let me in. Please, please let me in; I want
to speak to you!

AMANDA: Heaven preserve me from nice women!

SIBYL: Your own reputation ought to do that.

AMANDA (*irritably*):   Oh, go to hell!

> ELYOT *opens the door, and* SIBYL *disappears
> inside,* AMANDA *looks at* VICTOR, *who is standing
> with his back turned, staring out of the window,
> then she wanders about the room, making rather
> inadequate little attempts to tidy up. She glances
> at* VICTOR *again.*

AMANDA: Victor.

VICTOR (*without turning*):   What?

AMANDA (*sadly*):   Nothing.

> *She begins to wrestle with one of the sofas in an
> effort to get it in place.* VICTOR *turns, sees her, and
> comes down and helps her, in silence.*

VICTOR: Where does it go?

AMANDA: Over there. (*After they have placed it,*
AMANDA *sits on the edge of it and gasps a little.*)
Thank you, Victor.

VICTOR: Don't mention it.

AMANDA (*after a pause*): What did you say to Elyot?

VICTOR: I told him he was beneath contempt.

AMANDA: Good.

VICTOR: I think you must be mad, Amanda.

AMANDA: I've often thought that myself.

VICTOR: I feel completely lost, completely bewildered.

AMANDA: I don't blame you. I don't feel any too cosy.

VICTOR: Had you been drinking last night?

AMANDA: Certainly not!

VICTOR: Had Elyot been drinking?

AMANDA: Yes—gallons.

VICTOR: Used he to drink before? When you were married to him?

AMANDA: Yes, terribly. Night after night he'd come home roaring and hiccoughing.

VICTOR: Disgusting!

AMANDA: Yes, wasn't it?

VICTOR: Did he really strike you last night?

AMANDA: Repeatedly. I'm bruised beyond recognition.

VICTOR (*suspecting slight exaggeration*): Amanda!

AMANDA (*putting her hand on his arm*): Oh, Victor, I'm most awfully sorry to have given you so much trouble, really I am! I've behaved badly, I know, but something strange happened to me. I can't explain it, there's no excuse, but I am ashamed of having made you unhappy.

VICTOR: I can't understand it at all. I've tried to, but I can't. It all seems so unlike you.

AMANDA: It isn't really unlike me, that's the trou-

ble. I ought never to have married you; I'm a bad
lot.

VICTOR: Amanda!

AMANDA: Don't contradict me. I know I'm a bad
lot.

VICTOR: I wasn't going to contradict you.

AMANDA: Victor!

VICTOR: You appal me—absolutely!

AMANDA: Go on, go on, I deserve it.

VICTOR: I didn't come here to accuse you; there's
no sense in that!

AMANDA: Why did you come?

VICTOR: To find out what you want me to do.

AMANDA: Divorce me, I suppose, as soon as possible. I won't make any difficulties. I'll go away, far
away, Morocco, or Tunis, or somewhere. I shall probably catch some dreadful disease, and die out there,
all alone—oh dear!

VICTOR: It's no use pitying yourself.

AMANDA: I seem to be the only one who does. I
might just as well enjoy it. (*She sniffs.*) I'm thor-
oughly unprincipled; Sibyl was right!

VICTOR (*irritably*):   Sibyl's an ass.

AMANDA (*brightening slightly*):   Yes, she is rather,
isn't she? I can't think why Elyot ever married her.

VICTOR: Do you love him?

AMANDA: She seems so insipid, somehow——

VICTOR: Do you love him?

AMANDA: Of course she's very pretty, I suppose,
in rather a shallow way, but still——

VICTOR: Amanda!

AMANDA: Yes, Victor?

VICTOR: You haven't answered my question.

AMANDA: I've forgotten what it was.

VICTOR (*turning away*):   You're hopeless—hopeless.

AMANDA: Don't be angry, it's all much too serious to be angry about.

VICTOR: You're talking utter nonsense!

AMANDA: No, I'm not, I mean it. It's ridiculous for us all to stand round arguing with one another. You'd much better go back to England and let your lawyers deal with the whole thing.

VICTOR: But what about you?

AMANDA: I'll be all right.

VICTOR: I only want to know one thing, and you won't tell me.

AMANDA: What is it?

VICTOR: Do you love Elyot?

AMANDA: No, I hate him. When I saw him again suddenly at Deauville, it was an odd sort of shock. It swept me away completely. He attracted me; he always has attracted me, but only the worst part of me. I see that now.

VICTOR: I can't understand why? He's so terribly trivial and superficial.

AMANDA: That sort of attraction can't be explained, it's a sort of a chemical what d'you call 'em.

VICTOR: Yes; it must be!

AMANDA: I don't expect you to understand, and I'm not going to try to excuse myself in any way. Elyot was the first love affair of my life, and in spite of all the suffering he caused me before, there must have been a little spark left smouldering, which burst into flame when I came face to face with him again. I completely lost grip of myself and behaved like a fool, for which I shall pay all right, you needn't worry about that. But perhaps one day, when all this is dead and done with, you and I might meet and be friends.

79

That's something to hope for, anyhow. Good-bye, Victor dear. (*She holds out her hand.*)

VICTOR (*shaking her hand mechanically*): Do you want to marry him?

AMANDA: I'd rather marry a boa constrictor.

VICTOR: I can't go away and leave you with a man who drinks, and knocks you about.

AMANDA: You needn't worry about leaving me, as though I were a sort of parcel. I can look after myself.

VICTOR: You said just now you were going away to Tunis, to die.

AMANDA: I've changed my mind, it's the wrong time of the year for Tunis. I shall go somewhere quite different. I believe Brioni is very nice in the summer.

VICTOR: Why won't you be serious for just one moment?

AMANDA: I've told you, it's no use.

VICTOR: If it will make things any easier for you, I won't divorce you.

AMANDA: Victor!

VICTOR: We can live apart until Sibyl has got her decree against Elyot, then, some time after that, I'll let you divorce me.

AMANDA (*turning away*): I see you're determined to make me serious, whether I like it or not.

VICTOR: I married you because I loved you.

AMANDA: Stop it, Victor! Stop it! I won't listen!

VICTOR: I expect I love you still; one doesn't change all in a minute. You never loved me. I see that now, of course, so perhaps everything has turned out for the best really.

AMANDA: I thought I loved you, honestly I did.

VICTOR: Yes, I know, that's all right.

AMANDA: What an escape you've had.

VICTOR: I've said that to myself often during the last few days.

AMANDA: There's no need to rub it in.

VICTOR: Do you agree about the divorce business?

AMANDA: Yes. It's very, very generous of you.

VICTOR: It will save you some of the mud-slinging. We might persuade Sibyl not to name you.

AMANDA (*ruefully*):   Yes, we might.

VICTOR: Perhaps she'll change her mind about divorcing him.

AMANDA: Perhaps. She certainly went into the bedroom with a predatory look in her eye.

VICTOR: Would you be pleased if that happened?

AMANDA: Delighted.

    She laughs suddenly. VICTOR *looks at her, curiously.* SIBYL *and* ELYOT *come out of the bedroom. There is an awkward silence for a moment.*

SIBYL (*looking at* AMANDA *triumphantly*):   Elyot and I have come to a decision.

AMANDA: How very nice!

VICTOR: What is it?

AMANDA: Don't be silly, Victor. Look at their faces.

ELYOT: Feminine intuition, very difficult.

AMANDA (*looking at* SIBYL):   Feminine determination, very praiseworthy.

SIBYL: I am not going to divorce Elyot for a year.

AMANDA: I congratulate you.

ELYOT (*defiantly*):   Sibyl has behaved like an angel.

AMANDA: Well, it was certainly her big moment.

    LOUISE *comes staggering in with a large tray*

*of coffee and rolls, etc., she stands peering over
the edge of it, not knowing where to put it.*

ELYOT: Il faut le met sur la petite table la bas.

LOUISE: Oui, Monsieur.

ELYOT *and* VICTOR *hurriedly clear the things off
the side table, and* LOUISE *puts the tray down,
and goes back into the kitchen.* AMANDA *and* SIBYL
eye one another.

AMANDA: It all seems very amicable.

SIBYL: It is, thank you.

AMANDA: I don't wish to depress you, but Victor
isn't going to divorce me either.

ELYOT (*looking up sharply*): What!

AMANDA: I believe I asked you once before this
morning, never to speak to me again.

ELYOT: I only said "What." It was a general ex-
clamation denoting extreme satisfaction.

AMANDA (*politely to* SIBYL): Do sit down, won't
you?

SIBYL: I'm afraid I must be going now. I'm catch-
ing the Golden Arrow; it leaves at twelve.

ELYOT (*coaxingly*): You have time for a little coffee surely?

SIBYL: No, I really must go!

ELYOT: I shan't be seeing you again for such a
long time.

AMANDA (*brightly*): Living apart? How wise!

ELYOT (*ignoring her*): Please, Sibyl, do stay!

SIBYL (*looking at* AMANDA *with a glint in her eye*):
Very well, just for a little.

AMANDA: Sit down, Victor, darling.

They all sit down in silence. AMANDA *smiles
sweetly at* SIBYL *and holds up the coffee pot and
milk jug.*

Half and half?

SIBYL: Yes, please.

AMANDA (*sociably*): What would one do without one's morning coffee? That's what I often ask myself.

ELYOT: Is it?

AMANDA (*withering him with a look*): Victor, sugar for Sibyl. (*To* SIBYL) It would be absurd for me to call you anything but Sibyl, wouldn't it?

SIBYL (*not to be outdone*): Of course, I shall call you Mandy. (AMANDA *represses a shudder.*)

ELYOT: Oh God! We're off again. What weather! (AMANDA *hands* SIBYL *her coffee.*)

SIBYL: Thank you.

VICTOR: What's the time?

ELYOT: If the clock's still going after last night, it's ten-fifteen.

AMANDA (*handing* VICTOR *cup of coffee*): Here, Victor dear.

VICTOR: Thanks.

AMANDA: Sibyl, sugar for Victor.

ELYOT: I should like some coffee, please.

AMANDA *pours some out for him, and hands it to him in silence.*

AMANDA (*to* VICTOR): Brioche?

VICTOR (*jumping*): What?

AMANDA: Would you like a Brioche?

VICTOR: No, thank you.

ELYOT: I would. And some butter, and some jam. (*He helps himself.*)

AMANDA (*to* SIBYL): Have you ever been to Brioni?

SIBYL: No. It's in the Adriatic, isn't it?

VICTOR: The Baltic, I think.   ⟩

SIBYL: I made sure it was in the Adriatic.

AMANDA: I had an aunt who went there once.

ELYOT (*with his mouth full*): I once had an aunt who went to Tasmania.

AMANDA *looks at him stonily. He winks at her, and she looks away hurriedly.*

VICTOR: Funny how the South of France has become so fashionable in the summer, isn't it?

SIBYL: Yes, awfully funny.

ELYOT: I've been laughing about it for months.

AMANDA: Personally, I think it's a bit too hot, although of course one can lie in the water all day.

SIBYL: Yes, the bathing is really divine!

VICTOR: A friend of mine has a house right on the edge of Cape Ferrat.

SIBYL: Really?

VICTOR: Yes, right on the edge.

AMANDA: That must be marvellous!

VICTOR: Yes, he seems to like it very much.

The conversation languishes slightly.

AMANDA (*with great vivacity*): Do you know, I really think I love travelling more than anything else in the world! It always gives me such a tremendous feeling of adventure. First of all, the excitement of packing, and getting your passport visa'd and everything, then the thrill of actually starting, and trundling along on trains and ships, and then the most thrilling thing of all, arriving at strange places, and seeing strange people, and eating strange foods——

ELYOT: And making strange noises afterwards.

AMANDA *chokes violently.* VICTOR *jumps up and tries to offer assistance, but she waves him away, and continues to choke.*

VICTOR (*to* ELYOT): That was a damned fool thing to do.

ELYOT: How did I know she was going to choke?

VICTOR (*to* AMANDA):   Here, drink some coffee.

AMANDA (*breathlessly gasping*):   Leave me alone. I'll be all right in a minute.

VICTOR (*to* ELYOT):   You waste too much time trying to be funny.

SIBYL (*up in arms*):   It's no use talking to Elyot like that; it wasn't his fault.

VICTOR: Of course it was his fault entirely, making rotten stupid jokes——

SIBYL: I thought what Elyot said was funny.

VICTOR: Well, all I can say is, you must have a very warped sense of humour.

SIBYL: That's better than having none at all.

VICTOR: I fail to see what humour there is in incessant trivial flippancy.

SIBYL: You couldn't be flippant if you tried until you were blue in the face.

VICTOR: I shouldn't dream of trying.

SIBYL: It must be very sad not to be able to see any fun in anything.

AMANDA *stops choking, and looks at* ELYOT. *He winks at her again, and she smiles.*

VICTOR: Fun! I should like you to tell me what fun there is in——

SIBYL: I pity you, I really do. I've been pitying you ever since we left Deauville.

VICTOR: I'm sure it's very nice of you, but quite unnecessary.

SIBYL: And I pity you more than ever now.

VICTOR: *Why* now particularly?

SIBYL: If you don't see why, I'm certainly not going to tell you.

VICTOR: I see no reason for you to try to pick a

quarrel with me. I've tried my best to be pleasant
to you, and comfort you.

SIBYL: You weren't very comforting when I lost
my trunk.

VICTOR: I have little patience with people who go
about losing luggage.

SIBYL: I don't go about losing luggage. It's the
first time I've lost anything in my life.

VICTOR: I find that hard to believe.

SIBYL: Anyhow, if you'd tipped the porter enough,
everything would have been all right. Small economies
never pay; it's absolutely no use——

VICTOR: Oh, for God's sake be quiet!

> AMANDA *lifts her hand as though she were going*
> *to interfere, but* ELYOT *grabs her wrist. They look*
> *at each other for a moment, she lets her hand rest*
> *in his.*

SIBYL (*rising from the table*): How dare you speak
to me like that!

VICTOR (*also rising*): Because you've been irritating me for days.

SIBYL (*outraged*): Oh!

VICTOR (*coming down to her*): You're one of the
most completely idiotic women I've ever met.

SIBYL: And you're certainly the rudest man I've
ever met!

VICTOR: Well then, we're quits, aren't we?

SIBYL (*shrilly*): One thing, you'll get your deserts
all right.

VICTOR: What do you mean by that?

SIBYL: You know perfectly well what I mean.
And it'll serve you right for being weak-minded
enough to allow that woman to get round you so
easily.

VICTOR: What about you? Letting that unprincipled roué persuade you to take him back again!

> AMANDA *and* ELYOT *are laughing silently.* ELYOT *blows her a lingering kiss across the table.*

SIBYL: He's nothing of the sort, he's just been victimized, as you were victimized.

VICTOR: Victimized! What damned nonsense!

SIBYL (*furiously*): It isn't damned nonsense! You're very fond of swearing and blustering and threatening, but when it comes to the point you're as weak as water. Why, a blind cat could see what you've let yourself in for.

VICTOR (*equally furious*): Stop making those insinuations.

SIBYL: I'm not insinuating anything. When I think of all the things you said about her, it makes me laugh, it does really; to see how completely she's got you again.

VICTOR: You can obviously speak with great authority, having had the intelligence to marry a drunkard.

SIBYL: So that's what she's been telling you. I might have known it! I supppose she said he struck her too!

VICTOR: Yes, she did, and I'm quite sure it's perfectly true.

SIBYL: I expect she omitted to tell you that she drank fourteen glasses of brandy last night straight off; and that the reason their first marriage was broken up was that she used to come home at all hours of the night, screaming and hiccoughing.

VICTOR: If he told you that, he's a filthy liar.

SIBYL: He isn't—he isn't!

VICTOR: And if you believe it, you're a silly scatter-brained little fool.

SIBYL (*screaming*):   How dare you speak to me like that! How dare you! I've never been so insulted in my life! How dare you!

AMANDA *and* ELYOT *rise quietly, and go, hand in hand, towards the front door.*

VICTOR (*completely giving way*):   It's a tremendous relief to me to have an excuse to insult you. I've had to listen to your weeping and wailings for days. You've clacked at me, and snivelled at me until you've nearly driven me insane, and I controlled my nerves because I was sorry for you. I always thought you were stupid from the first, but I must say I never realised that you were a malicious little vixen as well!

SIBYL (*shrieking*):   Stop it! Stop it! You insufferable great brute!

She slaps his face hard, and he takes her by the shoulders and shakes her like a rat, as AMANDA *and* ELYOT *go smilingly out of the door, with their suitcases, and——*

THE CURTAIN FALLS.